Are the Mormon Scriptures Reliable?

HARRY L. ROPP

with revisions from
Wesley P. Walters

INTERVARSITY PRESS
DOWNERS GROVE, ILLINOIS 60515

Originally published as The Mormon Papers: Are the Mormon Scriptures Reliable? © 1977 by InterVarsity Christian Fellowship of the United States of America

InterVarsity Press is the book-publishing division of InterVarsity Christian Fellowship, a student movement active on campus at hundreds of universities, colleges and schools of nursing. For information about local and regional activities, write Public Relations Dept., InterVarsity Christian Fellowship, 6400 Schroeder Rd., P.O. Box 7895, Madison, WI 53707-7895.

Distributed in Canada through InterVarsity Press, 860 Denison St., Unit 3, Markham, Ontario L3R 4H1, Canada.

Unless otherwise noted, all biblical quotations are from the New American Standard Bible.

ISBN 0-87784-469-0

Printed in the United States of America

Library of Congress Cataloging-in-Publication Data

Ropp, Harry L.
  Are the Mormon scriptures reliable?

  Rev. ed. of: The Mormon papers, c1977.
  Bibliography: p.
  Includes index.
    1. Mormon Church—Sacred books—Controversial
literature.   2. Mormon Church—Doctrines—Controversial
literature.   I. Ropp, Harry L.   Mormon papers.
II. Title.
BX8645.R659   1987   289.3'2   87-3752
ISBN 0-87784-469-0

17	16	15	14	13	12	11	10	9	8	7	6	5	4	3	2	1
99	98	97	96	95	94	93	92	91	90	89	88	87				

Preface   7
Acknowledgments   9
Introduction   11

---

1.   *IS MORMONISM CHRISTIAN?*   15
God   16
Christ and Salvation   20
The Bible   25

---

2.   *THE BOOK OF MORMON*   29
The First Vision   33
The Origin of the *Book of Mormon*   34
Changes in the *Book of Mormon*   41

**3.   *THE BOOK OF MORMON &
NEW WORLD ARCHAEOLOGY*   53**
Is There Any Evidence?   55
Amateur Mormon Archaeologists   57

**4.   *THE BOOK OF COMMANDMENTS &
THE DOCTRINE & COVENANTS*   63**
Changes in the Revelations   64
False Prophecies   71
Contradictions between the *Doctrine and Covenants*
    and the *Book of Mormon*   74
The Lectures of Faith   76

5. *THE PEARL OF GREAT PRICE*   79
Revelation in the Book of Abraham   *80*
Book of Abraham Facsimiles   *86*

---

6. *WITNESSING TO MORMONS*   97
Where Should You Start?   *100*
Creating Doubt   *106*
What Should You Do Next?   *113*

Appendix A   Letter and Statement from the
    Smithsonian Institution   *117*
Appendix B   Book of Mormon Passages Reflecting
    Christian Teaching or in Conflict with
    Mormon Doctrine   *121*
Appendix C   Cross-reference between *Book of*
    Commandments and *Doctrine and*
    Covenants   *125*
Notes   *127*
Glossary of Mormon Terms   *135*
Selected and Annotated Bibliography   *137*
About the Author   *141*

Preface

Harry Ropp's Mormon Papers has for a decade served as a succinct and useful introduction to the complex topic of Mormonism. To have covered as much material as he did with such brevity and yet with clarity has been his unique contribution to Christians everywhere. Had his talented life not been cut short in the crash of his private plane, he would undoubtedly have kept this work up to date to the benefit of all.

InterVarsity is to be commended for seeing the basic value of this work and issuing this updated edition. Where I have found more recent and appropriate statements by Mormon writers, I have incorporated them into the text. Mormon admissions and attempted defenses in the area of American archaeology and the *Book of Mormon* have been briefly added. In a few instances I have expanded Ropp's points to take advantage of current discussions. One notable instance is in regard to Joseph Smith's attempt to translate Egyptian. Studies in that area have reached the point where it is now beyond any reasonable doubt that Joseph Smith was merely bluffing when he pretended to understand Egyptian by divine aid. Left largely untouched is the book's most helpful chapter on "Witnessing to Mormons."

In the appendixes, the most recent Smithsonian statement on the *Book of Mormon* has replaced that of the original edition. Passages from the *Book of Mormon* that support Christian doctrine, in opposition to present Mormon teaching, have been added to aid in witnessing to Mormons. The notes, bibliography and glossary have also been updated.

In the interest of keeping the book from expanding beyond its original compact size, a few items have been omitted. It is hoped that the deletions will not impair the usefulness of Ropp's original work. If this revised edition proves as serviceable to the Christian community as did the original edition, InterVarsity and all who had a hand in this project will be most gratified.

Wesley P. Walters

Acknowledgments

I wish to express my gratitude to Lincoln Christian Seminary for permission to publish my M.A. thesis in this expanded form. I also wish to thank Dr. James D. Strauss and Mr. Donald C. Smith for their assistance in writing the thesis and this book. My wife, Karen, has also contributed greatly through her active support of the project.

Harry L. Ropp

Acknowledgments

I want to express my gratitude to [illegible] for [illegible] permission to publish [illegible] ...
[illegible text, faded]
[illegible] which has also distributed [illegible] through her [illegible] collective.

Introduction

The first fifty years of the nineteenth century gave birth to several new religious movements and witnessed widespread growth among the various Protestant denominations. In 1817, Jemima Wilkinson, who thought she was the Christ, founded a religious colony just twenty-five miles south of Palmyra, New York, in a community named Jerusalem. Jemima's group became known as the Public Universal Friends. The Baptists entered New York State and began to split into small sects. Between 1814 and 1830 the Reformed Baptists, Hard-shell Baptists, Free-will Baptists, Seventh-Day Baptists, Footwashers and other Baptist groups were formed.

In the late 1830s the Methodists became the largest denomination in America, growing from less than 15,000 in 1785 to nearly 900,000 by 1839. The Presbyterians at the beginning of the nineteenth century were located mainly on the East Coast with some churches in Kentucky and Pennsylvania. By 1820 they had evangelized west of the Alleghenies enough to warrant the establishment of the Synod of Pittsburgh. As it began, this synod contained 216 congregations and 94 ministers.

In the midst of this religious ferment Joseph Smith grew to manhood. Young Joseph had moved with his family from Vermont to Palmyra, New York, about 1818. Between 1820 and 1830, Joseph laid the foundation for what has become one of the largest and fastest-growing religions in the world—the Church of Jesus Christ of Latter-day Saints, commonly called the Mormon Church. Beginning in 1830 with only six members, it has grown to an organization of about six million, with nearly 200,000 converts in 1985. This computes to over 500 baptisms per day during one year.

This expansion can be accounted for by the Mormon missionary system. In 1961 there were 10,300 full-time Mormon missionaries in the field; by 1969 there were 13,000. Presently the Mormons have over 29,000 full-time missionaries.

The Mormons have also experienced rapid growth in the British Isles and Europe. Africa and the communist countries are the only portions of the world that have not seen a similar Mormon advance.

It is the Mormons' success in proselytizing that makes this book necessary. In 1831, Alexander Campbell wrote the first able review of the *Book of Mormon.* At the end of that review, Campbell apologized for even taking notice of the *Book of Mormon:* "Such is an analysis of the book of Mormon, the Bible of the Mormonites. For noticing of which I would have asked forgiveness from all my readers, had not several hundred persons of different denominations believed in it. On this account alone has it become necessary to notice it, and for the same reason we must examine its pretentions to divine authority; for it purports to be a revelation from God."[1] Since Campbell made this statement, millions of people have made their way into Mormonism.

The purpose of this book is similar to Alexander Campbell's, namely, to examine the Mormon Church's claim to divine authority. Millions of people are in the Church of Jesus Christ of Latter-day Saints. If this Church is the only true church, as its missionaries assert, then these millions should be joined by millions more. But is the Mormon Church the only true church?

We are talking throughout this book about the Church of Jesus Christ of Latter-day Saints, whose headquarters is in Salt Lake City, Utah. Several splinter groups have formed from the original company led by Joseph Smith. The only other offshoot of major consequence is the Reorganized Church of Jesus Christ of Latter-day Saints, whose headquarters is in Independence, Missouri. Although there are many similarities between these groups, there are also significant differences. One should be sure to learn about these variations before attempting to share the information in this book with members of the Reorganized Church.

Many Christians today accept Mormons as brothers and sisters in the faith. This is an issue that must be dealt with immediately; so chapter one addresses the question, "Is Mormonism Christian?" After presenting conclusive evidence that Mormons are not Christians, we must next ask, "Are the extrabiblical scriptures the Mormons hold sacred really the Word of God?" We will examine the *Book of Mormon,* the *Book of Commandments,* the *Doctrine and Covenants,* and the *Pearl of Great Price* in that order (chapters 2—5). In the final chapter we will consider how to witness to Mormons. This topic comes last because a Christian who wants to witness effectively to Mormons needs to have a solid background in the Mormon scriptures. That forty people are won into Mormonism for every one that is led out bears witness to the difficulty of the task.

My hope is that those who read this book will not only be strengthened to resist Mormon proselytizing but also be motivated and helped to turn Mormons to the truth.

Chapter 1

IS MORMONISM CHRISTIAN?

Over the past several years Mormonism has been trying to gain acceptance as a Christian denomination. Historically it has been denied that position. In recent days, by downplaying strong doctrinal teaching and inaugurating extensive television and radio campaigns, the Mormons have reached their goal in the minds of many. Since people in general are not sure what it means to be a Christian and since the Mormons talk about Christ, Mormons are easily assumed to be Christians. But are they?

To determine whether Mormonism is Christian, we will consider its teachings on three of the most important Christian doctrines—the doctrines of God, Christ and salvation, and the Bible.

God

Who does the Mormon Church say God is? The first lesson of the Mormon missionary handbook *(The Uniform System for Teaching Families)* succinctly summarizes Mormon teaching: "God and Jesus Christ are separate and distinct persons, each with a glorified and perfected body of flesh and bones. . . . The Father and his Son, Jesus Christ, are separate and distinct individuals and not just different manifestations of the same person. . . . Their bodies are much like ours, but are glorified and perfected."[1] Thus the Mormons declare that God and Jesus are two different gods. Joseph Smith also taught, "In the beginning, the head of the Gods called a council of the Gods; and they came together and concocted a plan to create the world and people it."[2]

Mormonism has an answer to the age-old question of where God came from. Joseph Smith said,

I am going to inquire after God; for I want you all to know him and to be familiar with him. . . . I will go back to the beginning, before the world was, to show what kind of being God is. . . . God himself was once as we are now, and is an exalted Man, and sits enthroned in yonder heavens. . . . I say, if you were to see him to-day, you would see him like a man in form—like yourselves, in all the person, image, and very form as a man. . . .

I am going to tell you how God came to be God. We have imagined and supposed that God was God from all eternity, I will refute that idea, and will take away and do away the vail [sic], so that you may see. . . .

Here, then, is eternal life—to know the only wise and true God; and you have got to learn how to be Gods yourselves, and to be kings and priests to God, the same as all Gods have done before you,—namely, by going from one small degree to another, and from a small capacity to a great one,—from grace to grace, from exaltation to exaltation, until you attain to the resurrection of the dead, and are able to dwell in everlasting burnings and to sit in glory, as do those who sit enthroned in everlasting power.[3]

Mormons believe that God used to be a man but was able to learn how to be a god, and all Mormon men are planning on becoming gods just as they say our heavenly Father did. (The Mormons call this doctrine *eternal progression.*) Milton Hunter, a popular Mormon writer, explains further, "Mormon prophets have continuously taught the sublime truth that God the Eternal Father was once a mortal man who passed through a school of earth life similar to that through which we are now passing. He became God—an exalted being—through obedience to the same eternal Gospel truths that we are given opportunity today to obey."[4] God's earth-life, like ours, included a struggle to overcome sin. According to a Mormon study guide for training male leaders, the Father "was once a man, and has progressed, not by any favor but *by the right of conquest over sin,* and over death, to His present position . . . as the Supreme Being."[5] Brigham Young, the second prophet, seer and revelator of the Mormon Church, said, "Gods exist, and we had better strive to be prepared to be one with them."[6] One of the most famous statements on this subject was made by Lorenzo Snow, former President and Prophet of the Mormon Church: "As man now is, our God once was; as now God is, so man may be."[7]

Some Mormons even believe that God can be voted out of office for ungodlike conduct. W. Cleon Skonsen, a popular Mormon writer, states, "God's 'power' is derived from the honor and support of the intelligences over whom He rules . . . it follows as a correlary [sic] that if He should ever do anything to violate the confidence or 'sense of justice' of these intelligences, they would promptly withdraw their support and the 'power' of God would disintegrate."[8]

Mormons believe that God the Father has a wife with him in heaven. God is cohabiting with his wife and producing spirit-children who are then born into the bodies of earthly children. In other words, each of us is the result of two births, a spiritual birth in heaven and a physical birth on this earth. Both births are the result of sexual relations between each of our two sets of parents. In the second Mormon missionary lesson potential converts are taught, "Every person ever to be born on this earth lived in this premortal existence. We did not have physical bodies of flesh and bones as we now have. We lived as spirits—children of our Heavenly Father. . . . We testify to you that God is the father of our spirits, and that we lived with him before this life."[9]

Bruce McConkie, a prolific Mormon writer, Apostle and church apologist, states,

> Implicit in the Christian verity that all men are spirit children of an *Eternal Father* is the usually unspoken truth that they are also the offspring of an *Eternal Mother.* An exalted and glorified Man of Holiness (Moses 6:57) could not be a Father unless a Woman of like glory, perfection, and holiness was associated with him as a Mother. The begetting of children makes a man a father and a woman a mother whether we are dealing with man in his mortal or immortal state.[10]

On April 9, 1852, Brigham Young, the Church's Second Prophet and President, introduced the Adam–God doctrine into Mormonism. From him Mormons learned that God not only has a wife but is a polygamist, and that Adam and God are one and the same: "When our father Adam came into the garden of Eden, he came into it with a *celestial body,* and brought Eve, *one of his wives,* with him. . . . He *is our* FATHER *and our* GOD, and *the only God with whom* WE *have to do.*"[11]

In 1976 Spencer W. Kimball, the Twelfth Prophet and President, declared the Adam–God teaching "false doctrine."[12] This distinctive feature of Mormon theology has accordingly been officially abandoned. The question remains, however, Which Prophet taught the truth about God—Young or Kimball?

To summarize: Mormons believe that Jesus and God the Father are two distinct gods, both of them possessing glorified physical bodies. Besides these two, perhaps hundreds or thousands of additional gods exist in the universe. God alone was not responsible for the creation of our world but was just the head of a council of gods who planned the earth. God is merely a man who went through an earthly life similar to ours and became exalted through a system like the one Mormons offer people today. In other words, man came from God, who was a man, who came from another god, and so forth. Mormons can offer no ultimate cause for existence but only an endless series of births. God is not alone in heaven but has many wives. He is continually having sex with his wives to produce spirit-children to be born into the bodies of earthly babies. According to Brigham Young this god came to earth as Adam and began the human race.

The Bible answers Mormon doctrine in terms that cannot be misunderstood. Deuteronomy 6:4 says, "Hear, O Israel! The Lord is our God, the Lord is one!" Again, in Isaiah 44:6, 8, "I am the first and I am the last, And there is no God besides Me. . . . Is there any God besides Me, Or is there any other Rock? I know of none."

The New Testament likewise confirms Christian monotheism. Paul teaches in 1 Timothy 2:5, "There is one God." Occasionally Mormons will go to 1 Corinthians 8:5-6 to support their belief in many gods. But a close examination of these verses shows that Paul is actually asserting monotheism, not polytheism. Human beings may try to make gods out of many things, but that does not make these things truly gods.

Joseph Smith declared that both the Father and the Son have physical bodies as tangible as a man's and therefore they cannot dwell in a person's heart *(Doctrine and Covenants* 130:3, 22). God is merely an exalted man. But Jesus says in John 4:24 that "God is spirit." Adding to this Jesus' teaching in Luke 24:39 that a spirit does not have flesh and bones shows us we must trust either Jesus or Joseph Smith. We cannot believe both.

Christ and Salvation

According to Mormon teaching, Jesus Christ's spirit, like ours, was pre-existent. Therefore, we are all literally brothers and sisters of Jesus and of each other. Jesus, though, is set apart since he was the first-born of the spirit-children of God. *Doctrine and Covenants* makes this clear in 93:21-23: "And now, verily I say unto you, I was in the beginning with the Father, and am the Firstborn; And all those who are begotten through me are partakers of the glory of the same, and are the church of the Firstborn. Ye were also in the beginning with the Father."

If all of us, including Jesus, were born spiritually in heaven before we were born physically, what sets Jesus apart from us besides his being the first-born spirit? Mormons teach it is the manner of Jesus' physical birth that makes him different.

Matthew 1:18-20 says that Mary was pregnant and that the Holy Spirit was the cause of that pregnancy. The remaining verses in the chapter explain that Mary was a virgin and remained a virgin until Jesus' birth. Although Mormons claim to believe this, they persistently deny that Mary conceived through the Holy Spirit. Brigham Young stated, "Now, remember from this time forth, and forever, that Jesus Christ was not begotten by the Holy Ghost."[13]

Strangely enough, the *Book of Mormon* agrees with the Bible. In Alma 7:10 we read, "And behold, he shall be born of Mary, at Jerusalem which is the land of our forefathers, she being a virgin, a precious and chosen vessel, who shall be overshadowed and conceive by the power of the Holy Ghost, and bring forth a son, yea, even the Son of God." Yet despite the clear meaning of this verse, Joseph Fielding Smith, Tenth President of the Mormon Church, said, "They tell us the *Book of Mormon* states that Jesus was begotten of the Holy Ghost. I challenge that statement. The *Book of Mormon* teaches no such thing! Neither does the Bible."[14]

According to Mormon theology, God the Father, Jesus Christ, and the Holy Spirit are three separate and distinct individuals. So Jesus could not be the Son of the Father if the Holy Spirit was responsible for his conception. In order to make Jesus the Son of God, Mormons teach that the Father was responsible for the physical as well as the spiritual birth of Jesus. Brigham Young explained it this way: "The birth of the Savior was as natural as are the births of our children; it was the result of natural action. He partook of flesh and blood—was begotten of his Father, as we were of our fathers."[15]

An early Mormon apostle, Orson Pratt, explained how God could have sexual relations with the wife of another man and not be considered sinful:

It was the personage of the Father who begat the body of Jesus; and for this reason Jesus is called "the *Only* Begotten of the Father;" . . . But God having created all men and women, had the most perfect right to do with His own creation, according to His holy will and pleasure: He had a lawful right to overshadow the Virgin Mary in the capacity of a husband, and beget a Son, although she was espoused to another; for the law which He gave to govern men and women was not intended to govern Himself, or to prescribe rules for his own conduct.[16]

From these statements it is difficult to understand how the Mormons can refer to Jesus as having been born of a virgin.

And it is easy to see why this entire line of reasoning makes Christians shudder. This supposed Christian theology smacks of ancient pagan mythology and in no way accords with the God revealed in the Bible.

The Mormon view of Jesus' role in our salvation can be seen by referring to figure 1, "The Mormon Idea of Heaven." (This is a reproduction of a chart obtained at the Mormon Temple in Oakland, California.) The circle labeled "First Estate" represents the abode of God, the place in which we supposedly lived until we were born into an earthly body. At birth each of us entered the "Second Estate," or earth-life, which is a testing ground to determine where each of us will spend eternity. In other words, as one recent Mormon missionary handbook puts it, "Mortality is a probationary period during which we prepare to meet God again."[17]

From earth the way we go depends on us. The Mormons offer these options: The Telestial Kingdom, the Terrestrial Kingdom, and the Celestial Kingdom. Mormons teach that all people will go to one of them: "The gift of the resurrection will come to all men because of the death and resurrection of Christ. . . . Christ taught that we will go to different places after the resurrection, depending on how well we have kept his commandments."[18]

The "dishonest, liars, sorcerers, adulterers and whore-mongers," and the like, will gain the Telestial Kingdom for eternity. People who are basically good but are "blinded by the craftiness of men" and do not become Mormons will be sent to the Terrestrial Kingdom. A person who wants to end up in the Celestial Kingdom must go through a rigid system of works. Placing one's faith in Christ as Savior, repentance, baptism and receiving the Holy Ghost—referred to by Mormons as the "first principles and ordinances of the Gospel"—are merely the entrance to the Straight and Narrow Way that leads to the

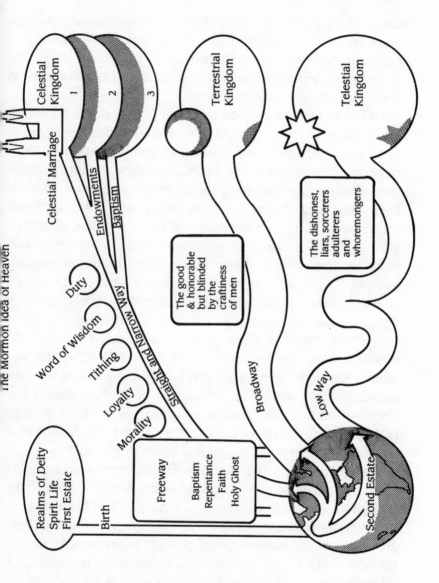

Figure 1. The Mormon Idea of Heaven

Celestial Kingdom. To attain to the Celestial Kingdom, temple work (such as celestial marriage, baptism for the dead and endowments) must be performed. Not every Mormon is able to get into a temple to perform these rituals; only Mormons in good standing can gain entrance.

To be a Mormon in good standing one must lead a moral life, be loyal to the Church, give a minimum of ten per cent of one's gross income to the Church, keep the Word of Wisdom (abstaining from coffee, tea, alcohol and tobacco) and perform other duties at the request of the Church. If a Mormon does not keep these ordinances, his local bishop will not give him a recommend (pass) to enter a temple. Every Mormon is responsible to work out his own salvation beyond what Christ has done for him. This is made quite evident in the missionary lessons: "The Lord has made you responsible for preparing yourself to enter his kingdom. Mr. Brown, do you feel that each person should be responsible for his own salvation?"[19]

The Bible, however, does not place us in such a position. The Bible declares, "By the works of the Law no flesh will be justified in His sight" (Rom. 3:20). It is futile for us to strive to make ourselves right with God; we cannot do it. Paul taught the Christians at Ephesus: "By grace you have been saved through faith; and that not of yourselves, it is the gift of God; not as a result of works, that no one should boast" (Eph. 2:8-9). The use of the perfect participle—literally "having been saved"—indicates that salvation precedes good works. Verse 10 then states that good works are the result of a life that has been remade by Jesus Christ. Good works cannot earn merit for us but they are the outward manifestation of a life made new by Christ. Christians indeed are commanded to live a life befitting their relationship to a holy God. But justification is by God's grace through faith. As Christians we have assurance that the shed blood of Jesus "cleanses us from all sin."

Unfortunately, the blood of the Jesus in which the Mormons believe is not that powerful. Brigham Young maintained, "It is true that the blood of the Son of God was shed for sins through the fall and those committed by men, yet men can commit sins which it can never remit. . . . There are sins that can be atoned for by an offering upon an altar, as in ancient days; and there are sins that the blood of a lamb, of a calf or of turtle doves, cannot remit, but they must be atoned for by the blood of the man."[20] Mormons in the time of Brigham Young practiced "Blood Atonement" openly. A number of Mormons who were accused of being apostates, adulterers or murderers had their throats slit to shed their blood and thus atone for their sins. Although Mormons do not do this today, they still believe there are some sins that are beyond the atoning work of Christ.

Even in modern times, however, a condemned criminal in Utah may choose the firing squad instead of hanging, thus giving a Mormon the option to have his own blood shed to accomplish atonement for sins not covered by the death of Christ. Brigham Young says, "There is not a man or woman, who violates the covenants made with their God, that will not be required to pay the debt. The blood of Christ will never wipe that out, your own blood must atone for it" (Journal of Discourses, III:247).

The Bible

When asked if they accept the Bible as the Word of God Mormons respond by quoting article eight in their Articles of Faith: "We believe the Bible to be the word of God as far as it is translated correctly." At first glance that sounds orthodox, but it does not accurately represent the Mormon attitude toward the Bible. Mormons quote much from the Bible. The King James is their favorite version and is, in fact, their only officially accepted translation. Despite their extensive use of the Bible, however, they do not really trust it.

Joseph Smith himself had reservations about the Bible. He once stated, "I believe the Bible as it read when it came from the pen of the original writers. Ignorant translators, careless transcribers, or designing and corrupt priests have committed many errors."[21]

The *Book of Mormon* reflects this same attitude:

And after they go forth by the hand of the twelve apostles of the Lamb, from the Jews unto the Gentiles, thou seest the formation of that great and abominable church, which is most abominable above all other churches; for behold, they have taken away from the gospel of the Lamb many parts which are plain and most precious; and also many covenants of the Lord have they taken away. (1 Nephi 13:26)

James E. Talmage, in his book *The Articles of Faith*, says,

There will be, there can be no absolutely reliable translation of these or other scriptures unless it is effected through the gift of translation, as one of the endowments of the Holy Ghost. . . . Let the Bible then be read reverently and with prayerful care, the reader ever seeking the light of the Spirit that he may discern between truth and the errors of men.[22]

Talmage says "there can be no absolutely reliable translation." The reason we cannot have a reliable translation is not that we do not have adequate scholarship but that the materials from which we must translate have been corrupted. Orson Pratt wrote, "Who knows that even one verse of the whole Bible has escaped pollution, so as to convey the same sense now that it did in the original?"[23]

The question then arises as to who made these changes. In 1 Nephi 13:26, the responsibility for them is placed on "that great and abominable church." In the *Missionary Pal*, Mormon Keith Marston suggests that the Roman Catholic Church is that "great and abominable church."[24] Being more direct in the *Di-*

vine *Authenticity of the Book of Mormon,* Orson Pratt states quite plainly that the "Romanists" are responsible for the corruptions in the Bible manuscripts.[25]

Mormon missionaries, as well as many other Mormons, quote the Bible freely, which is rather strange in light of their insistence that it is basically untrustworthy. In their proselytizing activities they imply that they wholeheartedly accept the Bible; but when presented with a contradiction between the Bible and Mormon doctrine, they refer to article eight in the Articles of Faith and say that the only reason there appears to be a contradiction is that the Bible is translated incorrectly at that point.

While the issue of the accuracy of the Bible text as we have it today may not be as crucial as the doctrines of God and Christ, it is nonetheless important because it bears on one's view of the final authority in religious debate. Christians have historically affirmed that each of the Bible's books "is inspired by God and profitable for teaching, for reproof, for correction, for training in righteousness" (2 Tim. 3:16), and few, if any, believe today that the Bible text has been so corrupted that it is an unreliable source of doctrine. The reasons we can have confidence in the accurate transmission of the original texts will be outlined in chapter six.

Thus, their views of God, of Christ and his role in securing our salvation, and of the Bible set Mormons apart from genuine Christians of all denominations. In fact, Mormons desperately need to know the way of salvation. But before we can share it with them effectively we must understand the problems with the Mormon system of belief. Who was this Joseph Smith, and why can we be sure the documents he produced were not divinely inspired? We will begin by discussing the origin of the *Book of Mormon* and the difficulties that stand in the way of affirming it as a revelation from God.

Chapter 2

THE BOOK
OF MORMON

There are several theories about the origin of the *Book of Mormon*. According to the official version, the year of 1820 was one of extensive religious activity in the area about Palmyra, New York, with the Methodists and Presbyterians holding revivals all over western New York. In this climate, young Joseph Smith found himself uncertain about which church was doctrinally correct. Early one spring morning in 1820 he decided to claim the promise for wisdom in James 1:5. He went into the woods to seek guidance about which church to join.

While he was praying, a pillar of light began to shine around him and he saw two people in the pillar. One spoke to him and said, "This is My Beloved Son. Hear Him!" When Joseph asked which of the sects was right, he was instructed to join none of them, because "they draw near to me with their lips, but their

hearts are far from me; they teach for doctrines the commandments of men, having a form of godliness, but they deny the
power thereof" (Joseph Smith—History 1:19).

This was just the first of several visions Joseph later claimed
to have had. The next was on September 21, 1823. This time
an angel appeared to Joseph and told him about some gold
plates he was to translate. These plates, the angel said, contained the "fullness of the gospel" as revealed to the former
inhabitants of this continent by Jesus Christ himself. The angel
also told Joseph that the Urim and Thummim, two seer stones,
were with the plates and were to be used to translate them
from Reformed Egyptian to English.

On September 22, 1823, Joseph Smith had another vision in
which the angel Moroni told him where to find the golden
plates containing a record of the former inhabitants of this
continent. A man named Mormon was largely responsible for
the content and preservation of these plates, the angel in-
formed Smith; thus, when they were translated by Joseph
Smith the book took on his name, the *Book of Mormon*.

When Joseph arrived at the place, the hill Cumorah, he
moved a large stone and thus uncovered a stone box holding
the golden plates, a breastplate and the two stones set in silver
bows (that is, like spectacles). He was prevented from taking
the plates from the box and was told he must undergo four
years probation before he would be allowed to remove them.
The plates were finally delivered to him on September 22,
1827, with this charge (in Joseph Smith's own words): "That I
should be responsible for them; that if I should let them go
carelessly, or through any neglect of mine, I should be cut off;
but that if I would use all my endeavors to preserve them, until
he, the messenger, should call for them, they should be pro-
tected" (Joseph Smith—History 1:59).

Not long after he received the plates Joseph and his wife

Emma moved to her father's home in Harmony, Pennsylvania, hoping to find a peaceful place to work on translating the plates. While in Pennsylvania, Joseph was called on by Martin Harris, a wealthy farmer from near Joseph's home in New York. Harris was so impressed with the work that he proceeded to assist Joseph in the translating. By June 14, 1828, Harris had written 116 pages of manuscript, as dictated by Joseph.

To convince his wife of the genuineness of the venture, he persuaded Joseph to allow him to take the manuscript home for her examination. While the manuscript was with Harris, it disappeared and was never recovered. Because the lost manuscript might have been altered, God, so Smith claimed, would not allow that part of the plates to be retranslated. Though Harris was never again allowed to help in the process of translation, he played an important part in financing the printing of the book and in the movement Joseph soon began.

Oliver Cowdery was the next scribe Joseph Smith used when he resumed the translation work in April of 1829. When the two men learned that the *Book of Mormon* taught baptism for the remission of sins, they went to the woods to pray about this revelation because Smith had never been baptized. On May 15, 1829, while they were praying, a heavenly messenger appeared to them and identified himself as John the Baptist. He stated, as he laid his hands on them, that he was ordaining them into the Aaronic priesthood, and that afterwards they should baptize each other. They were given the keys to the ministerings of angels and the authority to baptize for the remission of sins, but not the authority to confer the Holy Spirit by the laying on of hands—a gift they would receive at some time in the future. The messenger said he was acting in the name of the Messiah and under the direction of Peter, James and John, who held the keys to the priesthood of Melchizedek which would also be given to them later (Joseph Smith—History 1:72).

In June of 1829 the work of translating was completed. Up to this time, because the process of translation went on with Joseph and the plates behind a curtain and the scribe on the other side taking dictation, no one but Joseph had actually seen the plates. In the course of the translating, the record itself revealed that the plates were to be shown to others: "Three witnesses shall behold it, by the power of God, besides him to whom the book shall be delivered; and they shall testify to the truth of the book and the things therein. And there is none other which shall view it, save it be a few according to the will of God, to bear testimony of his word unto the children of men; for the Lord God hath said that the words of the faithful should speak as if it were from the dead" (2 Nephi 27:12–13).

This gave rise to "The Testimony of Three Witnesses" and later "The Testimony of Eight Witnesses." The three witnesses were Oliver Cowdery, David Whitmer and Martin Harris. The eight witnesses were Christian, Jacob, Peter and John Whitmer, Hiram Page, Joseph Smith's father and Joseph's brothers Hyrum and Samuel. (These two testimonies are still found in every copy of the Book of Mormon.)

Soon E. B. Grandin of Palmyra was hired to print five thousand copies of the book. The completed volume contained nearly six hundred pages came off the press in the spring of 1830. Thus, according to the Mormon Church, the Book of Mormon came into being.

To summarize briefly, the basic story of the Book of Mormon involves the migration of two groups of people from the Near East to the North American continent. The first migration was supposed to have occurred just before the confusion of the languages at the Tower of Babel. The second departure was from Jerusalem immediately prior to its destruction (in approximately 600 B. C.). A third migration was small and unimportant.

The story of the second migration and the resultant civilization comprise the bulk of the book. After arriving in North
America, these people divided into two tribes, one following
Nephi and the other his brother Laman. Eventually the Lamanites turned against God and warred with the Nephites. God
cursed the Lamanites with a dark skin. The dark-skinned Lamanites eventually killed all the fair-skinned Nephites and
were discovered by Columbus and called Indians. About A.D.
420 the last remaining Nephite prophet, Moroni, hid the golden
plates on which the Nephites' records were kept so Joseph
Smith could find them and bring them to light.

The First Vision

Since Joseph's first vision supposedly initiated his divine calling,
it deserves at least a brief consideration before we take an
extensive look at the revelation which came less than a decade
after it.

In recent years much information has come to light about
the official Latter-day Saints version of Joseph Smith's first
vision. Jerald and Sandra Tanner are responsible for bringing
much of the information available on Mormonism to light.
They are ex-Mormons who live in Salt Lake City just thirteen
blocks from the Salt Lake Temple. Because of their previous
connections with the Mormon Church, they have had access
to many rare documents and information to which others
would have been denied access. They have written in excess
of twenty-five books and pamphlets on Mormonism and printed them in their garage. In a recent book, *The First Vision
Examined,* the Tanners inform us that there are many conflict-
ing statements regarding this first vision.

According to Joseph Smith, he was born on December 23,
1805 (Joseph Smith—History 1:3). This would have made him
fourteen years old when he received his first vision, according

to the official account. The Tanners have reproduced a photocopy of a record of the first vision, dictated by Joseph Smith
about 1832, in which he states he was "in the l6th year of my
age." In this version, Joseph only relates seeing one person ("I
saw the Lord") while in the official account, written in 1838, he
says, I saw two personages." A photocopy of this differing narrative was published in the Spring 1969 edition of *Brigham
Young University Studies.*

The Tanners also have reproduced another description of
the first vision as it was told and recorded in 1835. In this
second unofficial narrative, Joseph Smith gives his age as
"about 14 years old," which is in harmony with the official
account. But he nowhere mentions seeing the Father or the
Son. Rather, he relates that he saw many *angels,* one of whom
forgave his sins and testified that Jesus is the Son of God. In
neither of the other two versions are angels mentioned. A photocopy of this version also appeared in the Spring 1969 edition
of *Brigham Young University Studies.*

Another important part of the official account of the first
vision is the date on which it took place. Joseph Smith indicat-
ed that a general religious revival in the Palmyra, New York,
area in 1820 led to his first vision. Wesley P. Walters, in 1967,
published evidence that there was no revival in the Palmyra
vicinity between 1819 and 1824. Not until fall, 1824, did such
a revival occur.[1]

These disparities make us wonder if Joseph Smith really had
a first vision or if he later elaborated on some "half-remem-
bered dream" or created a sheer invention to enhance his rep-
utation with the faithful.[2]

The Origin of the Book of Mormon
Not only is the first vision in doubt, but the source of the *Book
of Mormon* is not as certain as the Mormon Church would have

us believe. Several alternative explanations are live options. We shall examine the theories set forth by Fawn Brodie, George Arbaugh and Hal Hougey. Each of these three theories respond to Mormon claims and expose problems in the *Book of Mormon* text.

Fawn Brodie's Theory. In 1943, Fawn Brodie received an Alfred A. Knopf Fellowship in Biography. The result of this fellowship was *No Man Knows My History,* still one of the finest and most comprehensive biographies of Joseph Smith ever written.

Fawn Brodie was born and raised a Mormon and was the niece of Church President David O. McKay. She could not remember the first time she heard of Joseph Smith and his visions and his golden plates. "I seem always to have known him," she has said. The amount of research that went into her biography is staggering. The result of her efforts is the most authoritative work on the life of Joseph Smith available, one essential to any student of Mormonism.

Brodie's basic conclusion is that Joseph Smith himself was the author of the *Book of Mormon*. She considers Joseph to have been a genius and a born leader. Here is an example of her attitude after extensive research: "Scholars of American literary history have remained persistently uninterested in the Book of Mormon. Their indifference is the more surprising since the book is one of the earliest examples of frontier fiction, the first long Yankee narrative that owes nothing to English literary fashions. Except for the borrowings from the King James Bible, its sources are absolutely American."[3]

Brodie explains the content of the *Book of Mormon* from the historical setting of the author, seeing it as an "obscure compound of folklore, moral platitude, mysticism, and millennialism." The book was an attempt to answer those questions most in the minds of Joseph's contemporaries, especially about the origin of the American Indian, the secrets of the Masonic Lodge and Calvinism versus Arminianism.

Brodie suggests Joseph wrote the Nephite and Lamanite history first, but as discussion about the Indians' origin continued, the time span this history covered (namely, 600 B.C. to A.D. 400) seemed to him inadequate. Speculation that the Indians had migrated to this continent as early as the time of Noah was set forth in 1820 by Caleb Atwater. In 1823, Ethan Smith published *View of the Hebrews,* in which he quoted several Indian legends that were similar to the Old Testament flood account. Even the title of Ethan Smith's book suggests that Joseph was not the only one who had theorized that the Indians might have descended from the Hebrews.

To fill in the void, Joseph wrote the history of Jared and his descendants. They built boats described similarly to Noah's ark and filled them with animals, food and seed. Brodie points out that Joseph was careless in his choice of domestic animals, for he had them bring horses, swine, sheep, cattle and asses. It was widely known even in Joseph's day that Columbus had not found any of these animals when he landed in the Americas.[4] Joseph also, by the way, made the mistake of having the Nephites produce European wheat and barley instead of the indigenous maize and potatoes.[5]

Realizing there were imperfections in his work, Joseph sought to cover them with explanations within the book itself. Brodie cites three places in which this seems to be the motive behind particular verses. In one place, Mormon apologizes for having to use Reformed Egyptian because he had no room to write in Hebrew. This, he says, is the reason for the imperfections. In two other places, the *Book of Mormon* asserts that if it has any imperfections they are the mistakes of men.[6]

It is through Joseph's magnetic personality and his intuitive understanding of his followers that Brodie accounts for the visions Joseph's followers had. She labels this "the talent for making men see visions." Among these visions she includes Cowdery's seeing of John the Baptist and the viewing of the golden plates by the three witnesses and the eight witnesses.

One of the best examples of this talent is an account of the eight witnesses and their testimony to the existence of the plates:

The witnesses were "set to continual prayer, and other spiritual exercises." Then at last "he [Joseph] assembled them in a room, and produced a box, which he said contained the precious treasure. The lid was opened; the witnesses peeped into it, but making no discovery, for the box was empty, they said, 'Brother Joseph, we do not see the plates.' The prophet answered them, 'O ye of little faith! how long will God bear with this wicked and perverse generation? Down on your knees . . . pray . . . for a holy and living faith.' [After over two hours of prayer] looking again into the box they were persuaded that they saw the plates."[7]

One of the three witnesses, David Whitmer, later said that seeing the angel with the plates was like having "impressions." Martin Harris, another witness, said he saw the plates with his "spiritual eyes" and "that he never saw the plates with his natural eyes only in vision or imagination . . . as he saw a city through a mountain."[8]

Fawn Brodie sees the *Book of Mormon* as the product of one man, Joseph Smith. His genius alone accounts for its existence. All of those involved in the forming of the Mormon Church were victims of Joseph's powerful and persuasive personality.

George Arbaugh's Theory. George Arbaugh is so certain of the so-called Spaulding-Rigdon theory that in the opening pages of his work on Mormon revelation he declares that Sidney Rigdon was the founder of Mormonism and that Rigdon chose Joseph Smith to be its prophet.[9] The bulk of the information available on this theory has been collected by Charles Shook in his *True Origin of the Book of Mormon*. It contains affidavits and letters written between 1833 and 1900 which Shook organized and published in 1914. Arbaugh's section on the origin of the *Book of Mormon* uses Shook's book for most of its information.

The theory presents the Reverend Solomon Spaulding as the writer of a romance explaining the origin of the American Indians. He began to write this novel when he lived in Conneaut, Ohio, in 1809. In 1812, Spaulding and his family moved to Amity, Pennsylvania, near Pittsburgh, and there he turned his manuscript over to Robert Patterson, a local printer, to be published. Patterson had an employee, J. H. Harrison, who was a friend of Sidney Rigdon. Rigdon frequently lounged around the printing office, and when the manuscript came up missing, Rigdon was suspected of the theft. Rigdon reworked the manuscript with the aid of Smith and Cowdery, and thus we have what is known as the *Book of Mormon*.[10]

The affidavits and letters Shook gathered contain an abundance of material to support this theory. This evidence comes from Solomon Spaulding's immediate family, from other relatives, close and distant, and from other people who came into contact with his writings. Shook's collection also includes information that pertains to Sidney Rigdon and his whereabouts at crucial points in the story. Further, it has material that tries to establish contact between Sidney Rigdon and Joseph Smith before Rigdon's conversion to Mormonism in the early 1830s.

Fawn Brodie deals with the Spaulding–Rigdon theory in Appendix B of her biography. She denies the conclusiveness of the evidence Shook presents. She contends that Joseph Smith was himself capable of writing the book and that Rigdon could not have had any contact with Smith before 1830.

In Appendix B, Brodie gives a list of the activities of Rigdon from November 2, 1826, to November 14, 1830. There are several gaps of unaccounted-for time in Brodie's list—gaps which coincide with several important events in the life of Smith and his activities in translating the *Book of Mormon*. The first gap is from August 23 to October 9, 1827. This includes the date of September 22, 1827, when Smith claimed he received the plates.

Another gap occurs in Rigdon's activities between May and July, 1829. It was on May 15 that John the Baptist supposedly visited Smith and Cowdery. Some months later, Cowdery, on meeting Sidney Rigdon, was amazed at the similarity between Rigdon's voice and the voice of John the Baptist. In addition, during the first week of June, the translation was completed. While Brodie does not think this theory is correct, her own evidence can be construed as supporting it. Rigdon's chronology, however, was compiled by a member of the Reorganized Church, and the "gaps" in it may be due to incomplete research on the compiler's part. Furthermore the whereabouts of Joseph Smith during the gaps in Rigdon's known locations has not always been firmly established so that their meeting during those periods is more assumed than proved.

Hal Hougey's Theory. While Hal Hougey was not the first to set forth the similarity between the *Book of Mormon* and Ethan Smith's *View of the Hebrews*, he has, in his booklet *"A Parallel"—The Basis of the Book of Mormon*, enlarged the amount of information available.

Hougey shows that prior to Joseph Smith's publication of the *Book of Mormon* several books had advanced the theory that the American Indians were of Hebrew descent. Hougey also reports frequent newspaper articles on the subject to which Joseph Smith had access. It seems to have been a common topic of conversation. Joseph's interest in the matter is borne out by his mother: "During our evening conversations, Joseph would occasionally give us some of the most amusing recitals that could be imagined. He would describe the ancient inhabitants of this continent, their dress, mode of traveling, and the animals upon which they rode; their cities, their buildings, with every particular; their mode of warfare; and also their religious worship. This he would do with as much ease, seemingly, as if he had spent his whole life with them."[11] Such statements, according to Joseph's mother, were made by Joseph in 1824, several years before he translated the *Book of Mormon*.

Much of the information Hougey uses was compiled by B. H. Roberts, a prominent Mormon historian. After Roberts's death, his son made public mimeographed copies of his father's list of parallels between the *Book of Mormon* and Ethan Smith's *View of the Hebrews*. The list summarizes some of the major similarities discussed in a more lengthy manuscript Roberts wrote about 1921, but which has only recently been made available to the public. These are a few of the similarities:

1. Both set forth the Hebrew origin of the American Indian.
2. Both talk of an ancient book hidden—buried in the ground.
3. Both speak of prophets and seers.
4. Both mention the Urim and Thummim and a breastplate.
5. Both speak of ancient Egyptian inscriptions.
6. Both talk of a civilized and a barbaric element in the population.
7. Both have references to the destruction of Jerusalem.
8. Both talk of the gathering of Israel "in the last days."
9. Both quote extensively from Isaiah.
10. Both speak of a great gentile nation rising up in America in the last days to save Israel.
11. Both speak of the practice of polygamy among the early people.
12. Both speak of widespread ancient civilization on the American continent.

13. Both speak of an appearance of a white God on the American continent.[12]

Hougey says that *View of the Hebrews* was published seven years prior to the *Book of Mormon;* the first edition was printed in 1823 and the second in 1825. The book was published in Poultney, Vermont, where Oliver Cowdery lived before he moved to New York in 1825 and came into contact with the Smith family. It is therefore possible for Cowdery to have carried a copy of the second edition of *View of the Hebrews* with him to New York.

B. H. Roberts argues quite impressively that the *Book of Mormon* uses the same plot line over and over. It is therefore, he concludes, not beyond Joseph Smith's native ability to have produced the book by drawing on the pool of ideas circulating at the time and expressed in Ethan Smith's book.[13]

It is possible that elements of all three of the theories I have just described are correct. Hougey rightly states, "The possibility of Joseph's having used *View of the Hebrews* in no way precludes his use of other possible sources in writing the *Book of Mormon.* He may very well have used a number of sources."[14] In other words, Joseph Smith could have used his own natural genius and both the Spaulding manuscript and *View of the Hebrews,* as well as other materials, to produce the *Book of Mormon.*

Changes in the Book of Mormon

The most important claim made for the *Book of Mormon* is that it is the Word of God. If it can stand as the Word of God, then we would do well to study and accept it as such. Inherent in this claim is the claim to perfection Joseph Smith made for it when he stated, "I told the brethren that the Book of Mormon was the most correct of any book on earth."[15]

Joseph Fielding Smith, Tenth President of the Mormon

Church, likewise maintained,

> Inspiration is discovered in the fact that each part, as it was revealed, dovetailed perfectly with what had come before. *There was no need for eliminating, changing, or adjusting any part to make it fit; but each new revelation on doctrine and priesthood fitted into its place perfectly to complete the whole structure,* as it has been prepared by the Master Builder.[16]

In 1881 Oliver Huntington recorded that Joseph F. Smith, who became the Sixth President of the Mormon Church, stated in a sermon:

> Joseph did not render the writing on the gold plates into the English language in his own style of language as many people believe, but every word and every letter was given to him by the gift and power of God. . . . The Lord caused each word spelled as it is in the book to appear on the stones in short sentences or words, and when Joseph had uttered the sentence or word before him and the scribe had written it properly, that sentence would disappear and another appear. And if there was a word wrongly written or even a letter incorrect, the writing on the stones would remain there. Then Joseph would require the scribe to spell the reading of the last spoken and thus find the mistake and when corrected the sentence would disappear as usual.[17]

David Whitmer, one of the three witnesses to the *Book of Mormon*, gave a basically identical account of the translation in his *Address to All Believers in Christ*:

> I will now give you a description of the manner in which the Book of Mormon was translated. Joseph Smith would put the seer stone into a hat, and put his face in the hat, drawing it closely around his face to exclude the light; and in the darkness the spiritual light would shine. A piece of something resembling parchment would appear, and on that ap-

peared the writing. One character at a time would appear, and under it was the interpretation in English. Brother Joseph would read off the English to Oliver Cowdery, who was his principal scribe, and when it was written down and repeated to Brother Joseph to see if it was correct, then it would disappear, and another character with the interpretation would appear. Thus the Book of Mormon was translated by the gift and power of God, and not by any power of man.[18]

Most Mormons still believe that Joseph Smith was an unlearned man and that God did the translating through the stones.

Since God made the translation, we would expect the 1830 edition of the *Book of Mormon* to be exactly as God wanted it to be. It should therefore be the same in the current edition. But, in fact, there have been hundreds of changes. As early as 1898, Lamoni Call had counted two thousand alterations in what Joseph Smith called the "most correct of any book on earth." A more recent study by the Tanners has shown that at least 3,913 changes have been made in the *Book of Mormon* since it was first published.[19] Some 200 additional changes have been made in the 1981 printing, since the Tanners made their comparison.

The bulk of the changes are corrections of grammar or spelling, but some alter the meaning of the text. We shall look first at a few grammatical and spelling errors, then at some more substantive matters.

Like many who are not well-versed in grammar, Joseph Smith had trouble with the verb *to be*. Here are six errors from the first edition of the *Book of Mormon* which have been corrected in later editions. Since the first edition of the *Book of Mormon* was not divided into chapters and verses, the page on which each example is found follows the example.

1. "Adam and Eve, which was our first parents" (p. 15).
2. "and loosed the bands which was upon my wrists" (pp. 48–49).
3. "but it all were vain" (p. 142).
4. "it were easy to guard them" (p. 375).
5. "the words which is expedient" (p. 67).
6. "here is our weapons of war" (p. 346).

Another common mistake which later editions have repaired is the addition of unnecessary words. The following are five examples in which the word *a* has since been deleted from the original text.

1. "As I was a journeying" (p. 249).
2. "And as I was a going thither" (p. 249).
3. "Moroni was a coming against them" (p. 403).
4. "he found Muloki a preaching" (p. 284).
5. "the Lamanites a marching" (p. 529).

The first edition of the *Book of Mormon* uses many words incorrectly. It would be impractical to include them all here. To illustrate the variety of the errors, a list of eight of the most common ones is presented below. In each example the word used incorrectly is italicized and followed by the correct word in brackets. In each case the word has been corrected in later editions of the *Book of Mormon*.

1. "lest he should look for that he *had not ought* [ought not] and he should perish" (p. 173).
2. "having no *respects* [respect] to persons" (p. 224).
3. "I have *wrote* [written] unto you somewhat" (p. 377).
4. "they were *exceeding fraid* [exceedingly afraid]" (p. 354).
5. "they had *began* [begun] to possess the land of Amulon, and had *began* [begun] to till the ground" (p. 204).
6. "this he *done* [did] that he might overthrow" (p. 140).
7. "we have *took* [taken] of their wine" (p. 379).
8. "they did not fight against God *no* [any] more" (p. 290).

If we accept the mechanical view of revelation described above, we must conclude that God either wanted all the errors (or at least colloquial forms of English) found in the first edition of the *Book of Mormon* to be there or that God is not well-versed in the English language. Evidently the Mormons do not accept the first solution because they have proceeded to correct the errors. The latter solution is absurd.

While it is true that Joseph Smith made many of the corrections in the *Book of Mormon* himself, it is possible to show by comparing various editions of the *Book of Mormon* that many changes were made after his death. Dr. Sidney B. Sperry, a prominent Mormon apologist, admits that many of the changes were made by Dr. James Talmadge, a Mormon Apostle, and were first incorporated into the 1920 edition of the *Book of Mormon*.[20]

Mormons often rationalize that Joseph Smith had the right to revise his grammar and other mistakes in the *Book of Mormon*. If Joseph Smith were the author or even translator (by his own linguistic ability), then he would have had such a right. However, the original claim was that Joseph was only a tool used by God, and God himself was actually the translator. Therefore, neither Joseph Smith nor anyone else, for that matter, had the right to change God's translation.

It is one thing to correct God's grammar, but it takes a bold person indeed to alter the meaning of what he believes is God's Word. Yet this is what has happened in the following five cases. The Mormon Church made the first four changes to support a doctrine it developed at a later date, and it made the fifth to avoid an internal contradiction. Because the first four deal with the same subject, we shall consider them together and then look at the fifth.

The current Mormon doctrine of God is one of a plurality of gods. To understand this doctrine, we must remember that the

Mormons make a distinction between Jesus and the Father, claiming that they are two different gods. Jesus, they say, is Jehovah (the divine name, sometimes written Yahweh) while his Father is Elohim (simply the Hebrew word for God). In brief, Jesus, Jehovah, is the son of the heavenly Father, Elohim.[21]

But the founders of the movement apparently had no such doctrine in mind. The concluding statement in the "Testimony of Three Witnesses," found even in the current edition of the *Book of Mormon* reads, "And the honor be to the Father, and to the Son, and to the Holy Ghost, which is one God." Likewise, 2 Nephi 31:21 says, "And now, behold, this is the doctrine of Christ, and the only and true doctrine of the Father, and of the Son, and of the Holy Ghost, which is one God, without end. Amen." At the bottom of the page on which this verse is found in the 1961 edition is a list of six similar verses.

In the 1830 edition, in 1 Nephi we read, "And the angel spake unto me, saying: These last records . . . shall make known to all kindreds, tongues, and people, that the Lamb of God is the Eternal Father and the Saviour of the world; and that all men must come unto Him, or they cannot be saved" (p. 32). This extreme monotheism, where the Father is the Son, is known as Sabellianism. By 1835, however, the Latter-day Saints Church had abandoned Sabellianism and taught that there were *two* persons in the Godhead. At this stage the Father was "a personage of spirit" (that is, did not have a physical body) while the Son was "a personage of tabernacle" (that is, had a physical body). Consequently, in the 1837 edition of the *Book of Mormon,* as well as in all subsequent editions, the passage was changed to read: "And the angel spake unto me, saying: These last records . . . shall make known to all kindreds, tongues, and people, that the Lamb of God is *the Son of* the Eternal Father, and the Saviour of the world; and that all men must come unto him, or they cannot be saved" (1 Nephi 13:40).

The next two changes in the 1830 edition are made within the same conversation. "And he said unto me, Behold, the virgin which thou seest, is the mother of God, after the manner of the flesh. . . . And I looked and beheld the virgin again, bearing a child in her arms. And the angel said unto me, behold the Lamb of God, yea, even the Eternal Father!" (p. 25). This verse, in the same Sabellian manner, equates the baby Jesus with the Eternal Father. Since it did not square with developing Mormon doctrine, later editions of the *Book of Mormon* have changed the equation: "And he said unto me: Behold, the virgin whom thou seest is the mother of *the Son of* God, after the manner of flesh. . . . And I looked and beheld the virgin again, bearing a child in her arms. And the angel said unto me: Behold the Lamb of God, yea, even *the Son of* the Eternal Father!" (1 Nephi 11: 18–21). By the addition of the words *the Son of* the meaning of the verse has been changed.

Later the same chapter of 1 Nephi says, "And I looked and beheld the Lamb of God, that he was taken by the people; yea, the Everlasting God, was judged of the world" (p. 26). When this verse was printed in later editions of the *Book of Mormon,* it also contained the words *the Son of:* "And I looked and beheld the Lamb of God, that he was taken by the people; yea, *the Son of* the everlasting God was judged of the world" (1 Nephi 11:32).

Some Mormon apologists assert that the phrases in question were in the original handwritten copies of the *Book of Mormon* and were omitted by the printer. The Church Historical Department (an official arm of the Church of Jesus Christ of Latter-day Saints in Salt Lake City) has a portion of the original manuscript. It contains three of the four verses in question (the page that would have contained the fourth has not survived), and these three are in exact agreement with the first edition in omitting the words *the Son of.*[22] Joseph had his scribes produce a second copy so that, in case of theft, one would be preserved.[23] The Reorganized Church of Jesus Christ of Latter-day Saints has this second copy in the handwriting of Oliver Cowdery, which was made for use by the printer. In this manuscript two of the verses in question have the words *the Son of* added between the lines. Since this manuscript was marked up with the changes to be made in the second (1837) edition and the interlineation is in the same hand as the rest of the 1837 changes, the printer in 1830 clearly did not have these words in his text. In the other two verses nothing has been added, and they read exactly as in the first edition of the *Book of Mormon.*[24] This rules out the possibility of a printing error.

Often Mormons who are not aware of the existence of the handwritten copies of the *Book of Mormon* explain changes in the *Book of Mormon* by saying the printer who produced the first edition made typographical errors we should allow to be corrected. Comparing the original handwritten copies with the 1830 edition of the *Book of Mormon,* however, we see that the typographical errors were remarkably few for the country press that did the typesetting and proofreading. The late Mormon historian B. H. Roberts admitted this was the case. When speaking of the vast majority of the changes in the *Book of Mormon* text, he said,

> Such is the nature of the errors in question, and so interwoven are they throughout the diction of the book, that they may not be disposed of by saying they result from inefficient proof-reading or referring them to the mischievous disposition of the "typos," or the unfriendliness of the publishing house. The errors are constitutional in their character; they are of the web and woof of the style and not such errors as may be classed as typographical. Indeed, the first edition of the Book of Mormon is singularly free from typographical errors.[25]

The fifth example of a substantive change deals with a different subject. On page 200 of the 1830 edition of the *Book of Mormon,* the name of the king under discussion is Benjamin. In subsequent editions, the same section names the king as Mosiah (Mosiah 21:28). It would appear from the chronology in Mosiah 6 and 7 that King Benjamin had been dead for some time. Evidently, the leaders who were responsible for the second edition felt it was better to erase the error by changing Benjamin to Mosiah.[26]

Sidney B. Sperry, professor emeritus at Brigham Young University, has responded to the attacks on the *Book of Mormon* resulting from this change. Sperry says this was an inadvertent slip of the tongue on Joseph's part as he was dictating to Cowdery, or perhaps it was a mistake made by Mormon when he abridged the gold plates. Despite this, Sperry admits, "the reading 'king Benjamin' is an out-and-out error, because the king had been dead for some time."[27]

Neither of the two possibilities Sperry proposes fit well with the Mormon view of revelation. If we accept the first solution, we find that the *Book of Mormon* was not translated mechanically by the gift and power of God and may therefore contain countless errors. If we lay the blame on Mormon, we are in a similar dilemma because Mormon may have made other mistakes we have no way of detecting. Either horn of this dilemma is less than adequate to sustain the Mormon view of God-given revelation.

To escape the embarrassments that necessitated these various changes, modern, more liberal, Mormon apologists increasingly reject the mechanical theory of translation. B. H. Roberts was one of the first to suggest abandoning it. Roberts said Joseph Smith had to ponder over each part of the translation and then pray to ascertain its correctness, as Oliver Cowdery had been instructed to do. *(Doctrine and Covenants*

9 and *Book of Commandments* 8 tell how Cowdery was supposed to play his part in the translation process.) Therefore, Roberts concludes, "It is undoubtedly the manner in which Joseph Smith did translate the Book of Mormon through the medium of Urim and Thummim." Roberts further argues that since Joseph was used to thinking in poor grammar, he expressed himself in poor grammar. Then as Smith improved in grammar later in his life, he was able to fix his grammatical mistakes in subsequent editions of the *Book of Mormon*.[28] Fatal to this position is the fact that the *Book of Mormon* is written in imitation of the King James style. The Mormon Church has manuscripts written by Joseph Smith as early as 1829 and nowhere does he write in such a style. Therefore it is contrary to the facts to say that God merely enabled Joseph to understand the Nephite language and left him free to express this in his own style. There have been several more recent attempts to explain the changes in the *Book of Mormon*, but nearly all of them have followed Roberts's line of reasoning.

There are problems with Roberts's theory, however. It is built on two assumptions: that Joseph used the same method of translation as Oliver Cowdery and that the Urim and Thummim were part of this method. Both of these assumptions the *Doctrine and Covenants* and the *Book of Commandments* disallow. First of all, the portions of the *Doctrine and Covenants* that come from this period nowhere indicate that these gifts were the same for Oliver and Joseph. The text is also silent about Oliver's use of the Urim and Thummim. The verse Roberts quotes to show how Oliver used the Urim and Thummim (*Doctrine and Covenants* 8:2) does not mention them or even imply they were part of the process. On the contrary, it strongly suggests direct revelation: "Yea, behold, I will tell you in your mind and in your heart, by the Holy Ghost, which shall come upon you and which shall dwell in your heart."

Joseph Smith, on the other hand, states that the Urim and Thummim were very much a part of his translation work. In the writings of Joseph Smith, during his recital of the events leading up to his receiving and translating the golden plates, Joseph says this about the Urim and Thummim: "There were two stones in silver bows—and these stones, fastened to a breastplate, constituted what is called the Urim and Thummim—deposited with the plates; and the possession and use of these stones were what constituted 'seers' in ancient or former times; and that God had prepared them for the purpose of translating the book" (Joseph Smith—History 1:35). Several verses later he says, "I commenced copying the characters off the plates. I copied a considerable number of them, and by means of the Urim and Thummim I translated some of them" (Joseph Smith—History 1:62).

The translation process made use of the Urim and Thummim in a seemingly indispensable way. If we accept Roberts's theory that God through the Holy Ghost told Joseph the meaning in his mind and heart, then the stones become an unnecessary step in the process. Roberts's theory just does not fit Joseph Smith's claims.

Roberts's theory is an argument from silence. There is nowhere an account of the translation process that resembles the one he sets forth, yet there are several that describe the mechanical view of translation. We have already seen statements by David Whitmer (one of the "three witnesses" to the *Book of Mormon*) and Joseph F. Smith that attest to it.

With regard to Whitmer's statement about the *Book of Mormon,* it should be noted that Peter Whitmer, David's father, allowed Joseph Smith to live in the Whitmer home during part of the time Joseph worked on the translation. In *Address to All Believers in Christ,* Whitmer implies that one of the reasons he accepts the *Book of Mormon* as the Word of God is that it was translated in such a miraculous way.

Mormons try to discount these records by saying they are not official accounts. Whether or not they are official has nothing to do with their truthfulness. Whitmer's statement was printed in 1887, and Joseph F. Smith's was dated 1881. If these statements were incorrect, and were actually in opposition to the truth, why did no one respond to them before Roberts in the early part of this century?

Current Mormon apologists have no basis for dismissing the mechanical method of the translation process. This leaves the Mormons with their dilemma: Either Joseph Smith copied mistakes that were on the plates, which are not now available for examination, or the *Book of Mormon* was not translated by the gift and power of God and may, therefore, contain countless errors. Either way, this should cause even the most devout Mormon to question the integrity of the *Book of Mormon* in its present form and in its original construction.

Chapter 3

THE BOOK OF MORMON & NEW WORLD ARCHAEOLOGY

Since the Mormons—in several tracts and in the current missionary edition of the *Book of Mormon*—use archaeology to win many into the Mormon Church, we must take a close look at the archaeological evidence they claim supports the *Book of Mormon*. According to Joseph Smith, when he first learned about the existence of the golden plates, the angel Moroni told him they contained "an account of the former inhabitants of this continent" (Joseph Smith—History 1:34). This tells us the geographical area within which we should look for data. Let us see how the *Book of Mormon* describes these ancient people so we will know what kind of evidence to look for.

According to the *Book of Mormon*, each of the two waves of Jewish migrants built a large and prosperous civilization. The earlier one, which became extinct after a number of generations, had many farming utensils: tools with which to plow, sow, reap, hoe and thrash, and "all manner of tools with which they did work their beasts" (Ether 10:25-26). In addition, these Jaredites had "all manner of fruit, and of grain, and of silks, and of fine linen, and of gold, and of silver, and of precious things; and also all manner of cattle, of oxen, and cows, and of sheep, and of swine, and of goats, and also many other kinds of animals which were useful for the food of man. And they also had horses, and asses, and there were elephants and cureloms and cumoms" (Ether 9:17-19).

The later civilization, which endured from about 600 B.C. to A.D. 400, "multiplied exceedingly, and spread upon the face of the land, and became exceedingly rich" (Jarom 1:8). It "began to cover the face of the whole earth, from the sea south to the sea north, from the sea west to the sea east" (Helaman 3:8). The *Book of Mormon* names at least thirty-seven cities and recounts that in the final battle between the Lamanites and the Nephites, over two hundred thirty thousand Nephites were killed on or near the hill Cumorah (Mormon 6:10-15).

Not only was there a population explosion, but "the whole face of the land had become covered with buildings" (Mormon 1:7). Not only did the people build buildings, but they also made ships, temples, synagogues, sanctuaries (Helaman 3:14), coins of gold and silver (Alma 11:4), and weapons of war which according to Alma 43:18-20 were swords, cimeters [scimitars], breast-plates, arm-shields, head-shields, bows, arrows, stones and slings. Nephi describes one of the temples this way: "And I, Nephi, did build a temple; and I did construct it after the manner of the temple of Solomon save it were not built of so many precious things; for they were not to be found upon the land, wherefore, it could not be built like unto Solomon's temple. But the manner of the construction was like unto the temple of Solomon; and the workmanship thereof was exceedingly fine" (2 Nephi 5:16).

Is There Any Evidence?

If these accounts are true, then we should find ample archaeological evidence to support them. Ross T. Christensen, a Mormon anthropologist, admits that the *Book of Mormon* stands or falls on the historicity of its statements:

> The Book of Mormon is of such a nature that its validity can be submitted to a thorough and objective scientific test. . . .
>
> If the Book's history is fallacious, its doctrine cannot be genuine. On the other hand, if the historical content proves to be correct, by inference, it is impossible that the doctrine could be incorrect.
>
> . . . I am fully confident that the nature of the Book is such that a definitive archaeological test *can* be applied to it.[1]

We must now apply the test to which Christensen refers.

Mormon missionaries have often claimed that the Smithsonian Institution uses the *Book of Mormon* as a guide to its archaeological research. This claim is untrue. Appendix A contains a letter and statement the Smithsonian Institution has produced as a response to hundreds of inquiries made in recent years. To summarize, the Smithsonian Institution states that it has never used the *Book of Mormon* as a scientific guide and that Smithsonian Institution scientists see "no direct connection between the archeology of the New World and the subject matter of the book."

Joseph Smith claimed that the golden plates from which the *Book of Mormon* was translated were written in "Reformed Egyptian." If this were true, we would expect to find other examples of Egyptian writing in the Americas. The Smithsonian letter attests to the lack of any such evidence. In an article which appeared in *Dialogue: A Journal of Mormon Thought*, Michael Coe, who describes himself as "a sympathetic and interested outsider," discusses the Kinderhook plates, supposedly records in hieroglyphs discovered by Robert Wiley in

1843. Wiley reported he dug up the plates while excavating an Indian mound near Kinderhook, Illinois. When they were shown to him, Joseph Smith pronounced the hieroglyphs on the six bell-shaped brass plates to be the records of the descendants of Ham. About such archaeological claims Coe says, "Let me now state uncategorically that as far as I know there is not one professionally trained archaeologist, who is not a Mormon, who sees any scientific justification for believing the foregoing to be true, and I would like to state that there are quite a few Mormon archaeologists who join this group."[2]

W. P. Harris, one of the men involved in the supposed find, wrote in 1855 that Wiley had etched the hieroglyphs on the plates with beeswax and nitric acid. One of the original Kinderhook plates has survived and is in the Chicago Historical Society. George M. Lawrence, a physicist and Mormon by birth, had the metal tested at Princeton University. These nondestructive tests showed that it was a low-zinc brass or a bronze, that "the dimensions, tolerances, composition and workmanship are consistent with the facilities of an 1843 blacksmith shop and with the fraud stories of the original participants,"[3] and that the inscriptions were most certainly produced by the beeswax-acid etching technique. More recently a destructive test carried out by another Mormon scholar has supported the same conclusion as to the modern and therefore fraudulent nature of the plates.[4] So with this find discredited, there still have been no validated discoveries of Reformed Egyptian or Hebrew writing on this continent. Consequently, by identifying the Kinderhook plates as the writings of a descendant of Ham, Joseph Smith revealed his failure as a translator. As one writer put it, "Only a bogus prophet translates bogus plates."

Near the end of his article, Coe draws the following conclusion: "The bare facts of the matter are that nothing, absolutely nothing, has ever shown up in any New World excavation which would suggest to a dispassionate observer that the Book of Mormon, as claimed by Joseph Smith, is a historical document relating to the history of early migrants to our hemisphere."[5]

Brigham Young University Professor of Anthropology Dr. Ray Matheny expressed similar thoughts at a 1984 Sunstone Symposium. To an expert it looks as if the *Book of Mormon* "had no place in the New World whatsoever." It "just doesn't seem to fit anything . . . in anthropology [or] history. . . . It seems misplaced." The culture depicted in the *Book of Mormon* leads one to expect to find in the pre–Columbian Americas iron and steel metallurgy, wheeled vehicles, Old World crops such as wheat and barley, and animals such as horses and cows. Except for an "esoteric" or exotic occurrence of a wheeled toy and an occasional instrument of meteoric iron, these elements are totally lacking in New World sites. "It seems like these are anachronisms," Dr. Matheny said.[6]

Amateur Mormon Archaeologists

Despite the absence of archaeological support for the *Book of Mormon*, Mormons continue to produce a spate of archaeological works. Most are nonsense written by amateurs.

Not until 1938 did the first Mormon earn a doctorate in archaeology, and today only relatively few hold this degree. Many are honest scientists who study the facts and try to set forth the truth as they see it, even when it means raising a storm of protest from Mormon leaders. In reacting to the work of widely read but amateur Mormon archaeologists, John L. Sorenson, a Mormon elder who was assistant professor of anthropology and sociology at Brigham Young University, says, "Few of the writings they have produced are of genuine consequence in archaeological terms. Some are clearly on the oddball fringe; others have credible qualifications. Two of the most prolific are Professor Hugh Nibley and Milton R. Hunter; however, they are not qualified to handle the archaeological materials their works often involve."[7]

Dee Green, formerly assistant professor of anthropology at Weber State College, holds an M.A. degree from Brigham Young University in archaeology. He was a general officer of the University Archaeological Society and editor of the *U.A.S. Newsletter*. Agreeing with Sorenson, he states,

> Those volumes which most flagrantly ignore time and space and most radically distort, misinterpret, or ignore portions of the archaeological evidence are the popular Farnsworth volumes. Also inadequate, from a professional archaeologist's point of view, are the well intentioned volumes by Milton R. Hunter and a number of smaller pamphlets and works by various authors. . . .
>
> New World–Old World comparisons have been less popular but equally fraught with problems. The best known examples are the two volumes by [Hugh] Nibley which suffer from an overdose of "Old Worlditis." . . . He does not know New World culture history well, and his writing ignores the considerable indigenous elements in favor of exclusively Old World patterns.[8]

Keep in mind that these are Mormon scientists, not critical non-Mormon polemicists, making these statements.

The Mormon apologists being criticized attempt to show from available archaeological material that many of the anachronisms in the *Book of Mormon* are not anachronisms at all. Milton R. Hunter, for example, has attempted to demonstrate that the ancient Americans had horses prior to the coming of the Spaniards.[9] Although the Mormon Church takes no official position in such matters, many Mormons accept such "proof" without question.

Other popular Mormon apologists claim that the locations mentioned in the *Book of Mormon* can be shown on a map. In response to such claims, Dee Green comments,

There have been no spectacular finds (from the Book of Mormon point of view), no Zarahemlas discovered, no gold plates brought to light, no horses uncovered, and King Benjamin's tomb remains unexcavated. . . .

The first myth that we need to eliminate is that Book of Mormon archaeology exists. Titles on books full of archaeological half-truths, dilettanti on the peripheries of American archaeology calling themselves Book of Mormon archaeologists regardless of their education, and a Department of Archaeology at BYU devoted to the production of Book of Mormon archaeologists do not insure that Book of Mormon archaeology really exists. If one is to study Book of Mormon archaeology, then one must have a corpus of data with which to deal. We do not. The Book of Mormon is really there so one *can* have Book of Mormon studies, and archaeology is really there so one can study archaeology, but the two are not wed. *At least they are not wed in reality since no Book of Mormon location is known with reference to modern topography.* Biblical archaeology can be studied because we do know where Jerusalem and Jericho were and are, but we do not know where Zarahemla and Bountiful (nor any other location for that matter) were or are. It would seem then that a concentration on geography should be the first order of business, but we have already seen that twenty years of such an approach has left us empty-handed.[10]

As the position of Mormon archaeologists becomes clear, it is easy to see how John L. Sorenson could say,

In situations where sources of religious and secular authority conflict with each other, a Latter-day Saint sometimes finds himself in a quandary. He has been assured by a folklore transmitted in lessons, talks and church literature that archaeologists (usually Gentiles) are steadily proving the Book of Mormon authentic, while through his formal education and secular literature he has become aware that in actuality "the experts" seem to contradict the scripture.[11]

Sorenson has tried to overcome this Mormon folklore about *Book of Mormon* archaeology by writing a book of his own, *An Ancient American Setting for the Book of Mormon*.[12] This work limits the setting for Mormon lands to a small area in southern Mexico around the Isthmus of Tehuantepec. To do this he must minimize, ignore or rationalize the *Book of Mormon* material. This "limited geography" view was first suggested by B. H. Roberts when he realized that it was contrary to all scientific evidence to claim that the Hebrew *Book of Mormon* people gave rise to all the various tribes of the Americas. Sorenson, therefore, makes the Nephrites and Lamanites only a small minority among a multitude of other tribes of Mongolias lineage which, incidentally, are never mentioned in the Mormon scriptures.

The *Book of Mormon* represents its lands as surrounded by seas on the north, south, east and west. However, there are no seas north and south of Sorenson's site and the seas east and west are really oriented northeast and southwest. In Sorenson's reconstruction there must be two hill Cumorahs, one in Mexico and one in western New York. The greatest obstacle Sorenson faces, however, is from his own prophet Joseph Smith. Smith declared definitely by revelation that the *Book of Mormon* people landed in Chile and by the same revelatory power identified remains and ruins in Indiana and Illinois as Nephite settlements. Furthermore he declared that all the American Indians descended from the Hebrew immigration. In 1978 Mormon General Authorities sounded a warning against accepting theories of a limited geography, which "challenged the words of the prophets concerning the place where Moroni buried the records."[13]

The Mormons have made several attempts to show that some artifacts have been discovered that support the *Book of Mormon*. One of the most popular is the "Lehi Tree of Life Stone." In 1941 an expedition from the National Geographic Society and the Smithsonian Institution uncovered a stone monument in Izapa, Chiapas, Mexico, and designated it Stela 5, Izapa. Mormons first began showing interest in the stone in 1953 and have since maintained that the carving on the stela depicts the dream of Lehi, one of the *Book of Mormon* immigrants to this continent. M. Wells Jakeman has been one of the chief proponents of the theory.

Dee Green warns against accepting Jakeman's theory as proof too quickly, submitting that the only way we could know if the artist or artists had Lehi's dream in mind would be to ask them. At this point popular Mormon apologist Hugh Nibley agrees with Green:

> Science does not arrive at its conclusions by syllogism, and no people on earth deplore proof demonstration by syllogism more loudly than real archaeologists do. Yet Mr. Jakeman's study is nothing but an elaborate syllogistic stew. The only clear and positive thing about the whole study is the objective the author is determined to reach. With naive exuberance, he repeatedly announces that he has found "exactly what we would expect to find." Inevitably there emerges from this dim and jumbled relief exactly what Mr. Jakeman is looking for.[14]

Green adds that Jakeman's hand–drawn version, the one to which Mormons most frequently refer, was drawn from a photograph and not from the stone. Green examined the photograph, compared it to Jakeman's drawing, and concluded that the drawing is not accurate. Green further states that one should "not compare photo 109 in Ferguson's *One Fold and One Shepherd* nor the plaster reproduction of Stela 5 in the BYU Archaeology Museum since Ferguson's photograph is of the cast and the cast itself has been altered by Jakeman after his interpretation."[15]

Green refers to Thomas Stewart Ferguson. Ferguson founded the New World Archaeological Foundation, an organization through which Brigham Young University has conducted several archaeological expeditions, and he wrote three books trying to prove the *Book of Mormon* true on the basis of archaeology. But after publishing them, Ferguson decided he had not really found conclusive evidence and entertained doubts about all supernatural religion in the early 1970s.

Thus we may conclude with Ferguson and other Mormon writers that archaeology has not verified the *Book of Mormon.* Dee Green sums it up well when he says, "I strongly suspect that the Lord, at least for some time to come, will still require faith, not 'proof,'—and Moroni 10:4 ('he will manifest the truth of it unto you, by the power of the Holy Ghost'), not archaeology, will continue to be the key for those who really care to understand the contents of the Book of Mormon and desire to know its truth."[16] In other words, there is no objective, external verification for the *Book of Mormon.*[17] One must believe it by unsubstantiated faith. Chapter six evaluates this subjectivism in more detail.

Chapter 4

THE BOOK OF COMMANDMENTS & THE DOCTRINE & COVENANTS

If the Book of Mormon were the only extrabiblical revelation claimed by the Mormon Church, Mormon theology would have few major differences from orthodox Christianity. But the Mormon Church takes very few of its doctrines from the *Book of Mormon.* Some of the teachings most vital and most peculiar to Mormonism not found in the *Book of Mormon* are (1) the organizational structure of the church, (2) the Melchizedek priesthood, (3) the Aaronic priesthood, (4) the plurality of gods, (5) God as an exalted man, (6) a human being's ability to become a god, (7) the three degrees of heaven, (8) the plurality of wives, (9) the Word of Wisdom, (10) the pre-existence of the human spirit, (11) eternal progression, (12) baptism for the dead and (13) celestial marriage.[1]

The main source of these doctrines is either the *Book of Commandments* or the *Doctrine and Covenants*. The *Book of Commandments* deals with the early organizational structure of the Church, while the *Doctrine and Covenants* mentions or implies all of them. The *Book of Commandments,* the first published collection of the revelations Joseph Smith received during and after the translation of the *Book of Mormon,* was printed in 1833 and then enlarged and reprinted in 1835 under the title *Doctrine and Covenants.* While the *Book of Commandments* contains only the sixty-five revelations that came between July 1828 and September 1831, the *Doctrine and Covenants* contains an additional seventy-one sections. A comparison of the two documents reveals that drastic changes have been made from the one to the other. Some verses are rewritten; some are omitted; others are added. Yet both books claim to be the Word of God:

> Search these commandments, for they are true and faithful, and the prophecies and promises which are in them shall all be fulfilled. What I the Lord have spoken, I have spoken, and I excuse not myself; and though the heavens and the earth pass away, my word shall not pass away, but shall all be fulfilled, whether by my own voice or by the voice of my servants, it is the same. For behold, and lo, the Lord is God, and the Spirit beareth record, and the record is true, and the truth abideth forever and ever. Amen. (*Book of Commandments* 1:7; *Doctrine and Covenants* 1:37–39)

Changes in the Revelations

Why the differences between the two books? Some of the revelations were added to support doctrines Joseph Smith had begun teaching. Other revelations were expanded to make new doctrines seem to have an earlier origin than they in fact had.

Some of the initial revelations contained statements that contradicted later doctrines, and so parts of them were omitted.
Several specific cases will illustrate the nature of the changes:

1. At least fifty changes have been made in the first four
verses of the fourth chapter of *Book of Commandments*. One
in particular, 4:2, will concern us: "He [Joseph Smith] has no
power over them [the gold plates] except I grant it unto him;
and he has a gift to translate the book, and I have commanded
him that he shall pretend to no other gift, for I will grant him
no other gift." Here Joseph was claiming, first, that his gift to
translate the plates was from God, and second, that this was
the only gift he was to receive.

Had Joseph heeded this revelation, he would have stopped
writing scripture when he finished the *Book of Mormon*. Later,
however, when he began to compile the revelations, those familiar with them argued that God never meant them to be
printed.[2] Joseph continued to force the issue until he won out,
and the reason for his insistence soon became clear: he, Rigdon
and a few others were to receive the profits from the book's
sale, as a reward for their hard work (*Doctrine and Covenants*
70:5–8, 15–18).

After the printing of the *Book of Commandments,* Joseph
apparently realized that the very existence of the book was a
contradiction of *Book of Commandments* 4:2. If this verse was
left in its original form, then it would be obvious that those who
opposed the printing had been right and Joseph had been
wrong. The verse as it now stands in *Doctrine and Covenants*
5:4 reads this way (the italicized words are the words that have
either been added or changed in some way since the original
printing): "And *you have* a gift to translate the *plates; and this
is the first gift that I bestowed upon you;* and I have commanded that *you should* pretend to no other gift *until my purpose is fulfilled in this;* for I will grant *unto you* no other gift *until*

it is finished." These changes reverse the meaning of the original version. By making them, Joseph opened the door for further additions to be made to the scripture of his church.

2. *Book of Commandments* 6, when published in 1833, contained 143 words. When reprinted this alleged translation of an ancient parchment (*Doctrine and Covenants* 7:1-3), had grown to 252 words. The preface to this chapter in the *Book of Commandments* indicates it is a translation through the Urim and Thummim of a "parchment, written and hid up" by the apostle John. It is this claim that creates the most difficult problem. How could a translation expand by 109 words? The Tanners suggest there are only three possible explanations: (1) The Lord may have revealed to Joseph that the first translation was incorrect and that many words had been left out. This would cast doubt on Joseph's ability as a translator and hence on his other translations. (2) Before reprinting this translation, Joseph Smith decided to attribute words to John which John did not write. This would make Joseph a deceiver. (3) Joseph contrived the entire revelation but suppressed part of it in the first printing only to add it two years later. This, too, would make Joseph a deceiver.[3]

3. In June 1829, Joseph Smith received instructions about the new church he was to establish. The structure of this new church was to be found in the "fullness of the gospel" as it had been revealed in the *Book of Mormon:* "You rely upon the things which are written; for in them are all things written, concerning my church, my gospel, and my rock. Wherefore if you shall build up my church, and my gospel, and my rock, the gates of hell shall not prevail against you" (*Book of Commandments* 15:3-4).

This verse does not mention the *Book of Mormon* by name but refers instead to "the things which are written." The introduction to this revelation says it was given to Oliver Cowdery while he was acting as scribe for Joseph Smith. In verses 2 and 3 of this revelation God tells Oliver that the things he has written—that is, the *Book of Mormon*—are true; therefore, he should rely on them.

Many Mormons claim that the "things written" include all revelation from God. This cannot be supported from the context. Sidney B. Sperry, in his *Doctrine and Covenants Compendium,* says that the "things written" are "doubtless in the *Book of Mormon.*"[4] We would expect, therefore, to find all the doctrines, offices and structures of the Mormon Church in the *Book of Mormon.*

But, as noted at the beginning of this chapter, such is not the case. The *Book of Mormon* does not teach many of the Church's doctrines, nor does it contain most of the Church's offices or structures. If Joseph's early revelation about the new church he was to establish were true, and the *Book of Mormon* contained all that is necessary for the Latter-day Saints Church, then the Church would have to deny all of the thirteen doctrines we listed.

Recognizing this problem, Joseph Smith solved it by rewriting the revelation to allow for future revelation. When reprinted in *Doctrine and Covenants,* the passage quoted above from the *Book of Commandments* read, "You rely upon the things which are written; for in them are all things written concerning *the foundation of* my church, my gospel, and my rock. Wherefore, if you shall build up my church, *upon the foundation* of my gospel and my rock, the gates of hell shall not prevail against you" (*Doctrine and Covenants* 18:3-5). The word *foundation* has been inserted twice, which changes the meaning of the revelation. The *Book of Mormon* no longer contains "all things" about the Church, but now only the "foundation" of the Church. Thus, Joseph Smith made it possible for additional doctrines to be revealed.[5]

4. In August of 1830, Sidney Rigdon broke off relations with Alexander Campbell over the issue of re-establishing a communal society in the Disciples of Christ churches. On his own, Rigdon began a communal society at Kirtland, Ohio, near Cleveland. Not long after the split, Mormon missionaries arrived in Kirtland, and in less than three weeks Rigdon and his whole community had become Mormons.[6]

In February of the following year, 1831, a revelation was received that gave the Lord's endorsement to the communal effort. The passage about communal life is found in the middle of a rather lengthy revelation on the "law for the governing of the church." *Book of Commandments* 44:26–29 describes how "all" the properties of the church members are to be consecrated to the Church and given to each "as he stands in need."

By the time the *Doctrine and Covenants* was printed, the Mormon communal society had failed. It was necessary to alter only a few words of the revelation to shift its meaning. The word *all* was changed to *of,* so the phrase in which it was included now reads in *Doctrine and Covenants* 42:30, "And behold, thou wilt *remember the poor,* and consecrate *of* thy properties *for their support."* The words *remember the poor* and *for their support* were added to make the poor, and not every member of the Church, the recipients of the consecrated goods. The passage has shifted from being the ground rules of a communal society to being those of a church welfare program, clearly an attempt to hide the communal ideals present in the Kirtland Church.

5. Several changes have been made in the revelations concerning the priesthood. David Whitmer, one of the three witnesses to the *Book of Mormon,* rebelled against these changes and made the following statement about instituting the high priesthood: "The office of high priests was never spoken of, and never thought of being established in the church until Rigdon

came in. Remember that we had been preaching from August, 1829, until June, 1831—almost two years—and had baptized about 2,000 members into the Church of Christ, and had not one high priest."[7]

Whitmer further related that "Brother Joseph" had often referred to "elder" as being the highest office in the Mormon Church. As implied in the quote, Whitmer credited Rigdon with having introduced the high, or Melchizedek, priesthood into the Latter-day Saints Church, claiming that Rigdon would expound to Joseph the Old Testament Scriptures about the high priest and the priesthood and would persuade Joseph to inquire of the Lord about them. Promptly, Joseph would receive a revelation sustaining the view Rigdon had set forth. In this way the high priesthood entered the Latter-day Saints Church.

Book of Commandments 28, a revelation given on September 4, 1830, contains seven short verses with a total of twenty-three lines. Its general theme is the "sacrament" (the Mormon term for the Lord's Supper), and nowhere does it mention the priesthood. The parallel passage in *Doctrine and Covenants* 27:1-18 has eighteen verses and more than twice the number of words than the original version. It prescribes two ordinations: (1) the ordination into the Aaronic priesthood and (2) the ordination to apostleship by Peter, James and John. Mormon apologists today claim this second ordination was to confer the Melchizedek priesthood.[8] The strange feature about this crucial preisthood insertion is that it is placed directly in the middle of a sentence! In verse 6 of the *Book of Commandments* (27:5 in the present edition) Christ tells the Mormon Church "I will drink of the fruit of the vine with you on the earth, and with . . ." At this point eight verses on the priesthood are inserted and it is only at verse 14 of the present edition that the original sentence concludes—"all those whom my Father hath given me." Such haphazard insertions hardly can be regarded as a *true* revelation from an unerring God.

With regard to the priesthood, the following changes were also made in later editions of *Doctrine and Covenants:* (1) *Book of Commandments* 24:44-45 makes no mention of these offices: presiding elders, traveling bishops, high counselors, high priests and presidents of the high priesthood. *Doctrine and Covenants* 20:49-68 adds all of them. (2) *Book of Commandments* 44:26-29 makes no mention of high priests, high councils, or counselors, but *Doctrine and Covenants* 42:31-34 includes them. (3) *Book of Commandments* 44:54-55 makes no mention of high priests, counselors or bishops, but *Doctrine and Covenants* 42:62-73 has all three, equating the elders with high priests.

We have not examined all of the changes that have been made in the *Book of Commandments,* but we have seen enough to know that these supposed revelations from God do not measure up to the standard they set for themselves. They do not fulfill the claim that "though the heavens and the earth pass away, my word shall not pass away" and that "the record is true, and the truth abideth forever and ever. Amen."

To admit that the changes were made by Joseph Smith would be to admit that God is not their author. To claim that God authorized the changes presents other problems. For God to change his mind and reverse his position on matters of doctrine is hard to conceive. Joseph Smith would have us believe, for instance, that (1) at one time God said the *Book of Mormon* was all that was necessary for the restoration of the Church but later decided it was not enough; (2) once God said Joseph's only gift was the ability to translate the gold plates, but then chose to make that only the first endowment; and (3) God first commanded the Mormons to establish a communal society, but changed his design to a welfare program when the communal effort failed. Apparently, it is not just that God has given new revelation for a new age but that he or his prophets have "rewritten" the old revelation so that it squares with the new ideas. Mormon writers are constantly seeking ways of rationalizing why God would alter his ideas just two years after they were first published to the world. This is difficult enough to explain. But to present these alterations under the original date as though they were a part of the original revelation makes God a party to misrepresentation. It is easier to attribute this doctoring of the records to man rather than God. We must conclude that the revelations on which the essential Mormon doctrines are based originated not with God, but with Joseph Smith.

False Prophecies

While many of the revelations recorded in the *Doctrine and Covenants* were commands, some of them were predictions about the future. We shall look at two of the several prophecies Joseph Smith made that did not come to pass. The first one concerns the building of a temple and the gathering of Israel. The second is about the Civil War.

In *Doctrine and Covenants* 84:2-5 and 31 prophecy projects the building of a city called New Jerusalem and a temple. This new city and temple were to be built "in this generation . . . in the western boundaries of the State of Missouri, and dedicated by the hand of Joseph Smith." The sons of Moses and Aaron, it was foretold, would "offer an acceptable offering and sacrifice in the house of the Lord, which house shall be built unto the Lord in this generation."

This prophecy was given on September 22 and 23, 1832. At that time the Mormons were anticipating a move to western Missouri, though they did not begin their major move to Missouri in large numbers until 1836. In 1838 Joseph Smith and his chief lieutenants moved to Missouri when they were forced out of Kirtland. After severe persecution, the Mormons were driven from Missouri in early 1839. They fled to Quincy, Illinois, and never had a chance to build in Missouri the temple they had anticipated erecting.[9]

The prophecy contained things that were not and cannot now be fulfilled. Not only was a temple never built in the western part of Missouri, but the only generation that could have built it is now dead. Furthermore, the temple was not dedicated by Joseph Smith and the city of New Jerusalem was not established.

One reason it is not possible for Mormon apologists to pull this prophecy out of its time limitations is that Joseph Smith did prepare to build the temple in question—a marker-stone was laid and building plans drawn up—but he never completed it. Both the original set of drawings and a revised set are in the Church archives. While God was supposedly giving guidance for these plans to Joseph Smith in Kirtland, Ohio, he was apparently unaware that the Mormons were being driven out of Independence, Missouri, where the building site had been divinely laid out. Mormon apologists have tried to extend the length of a generation to 125 years so that the prophecy could be fulfilled.[10] But this effort was abandoned when Joseph Fielding Smith admitted that no one who was in the Church when this revelation was given remained alive.[11]

Another false prophecy, found in *Doctrine and Covenants* 87, concerns the Civil War. The details of the revelation are (1) the rebellion would begin in South Carolina; (2) it would shortly come to pass; (3) "war will be poured out upon all nations, beginning at this place"; (4) slaves would rebel against their masters; (5) famine, plague and earthquake would come from God; and (6) all nations would come to an end. This prophecy was given on December 25, 1832.

The Tanners have shown that Joseph Smith, prior to receiving this revelation, could have known that President Andrew Jackson had alerted the nation's troops in response to South Carolina's declaring a tariff act null and void.[12] The nation was fully expecting a civil war to begin promptly in South Carolina. This fact is borne out by a story in the February 1833 edition of the Mormon monthly, *The Evening and the Morning Star*, in an article titled "Rebellion in South Carolina." This article stated, "In addition to the above tribulations, South Carolina has rebelled against the laws of the United States; held a state convention, and passed ordinances, the same as declaring herself an independent nation." The article further reported that Jackson had ordered several companies of artillery to Charleston to prepare for the war that seemed imminent. Since *The Evening and the Morning Star* was a monthly publication, the news could have been available to Joseph as much as a month before the printing of this story. The idea of an impending civil war was not original to him.

The revelation stated that these events were to come to pass shortly, yet not until 1861 did South Carolina actually secede from the Union and the war begin. It foretold, too, that war would be "poured out upon all nations," yet the Civil War did not evolve into a worldwide conflict. Also, the Civil War did not result in the "end of all nations."

Was Joseph Smith a prophet of God? In the *Inspired Version of the Holy Scriptures*, the version on which Joseph Smith himself put his seal of approval, Deuteronomy 18:20–22 reads (just as it does in the King James):

But the prophet, which shall presume to speak a word in my name, which I have not commanded him to speak, or that shall speak in the name of other gods, even that prophet shall die. And if thou say in thine heart, How shall we know the word which the Lord hath not spoken? When a prophet speaketh in the name of the Lord, if the thing follow not, nor come to pass, that is the thing which the Lord hath not spoken, but the prophet hath spoken it presumptuously: thou shalt not be afraid of him.

On the basis of Scripture, Joseph Smith cannot stand as a true prophet, for when a true prophet gives God's word, it cannot fail to come to pass.

Contradictions between the *Doctrine and Covenants* and the *Book of Mormon*

Several of the revelations in the *Doctrine and Covenants* contradict the teachings in the *Book of Mormon*. One example concerns the purpose of baptism and its relation to forgiveness of sins and the gift of the Holy Spirit; the other, plural marriage.

1. *Doctrine and Covenants* 20:37 indicates that those who repent of their sins and show by works that they have received the Holy Spirit "shall be received by baptism into his church."[13] It is the order of events that is important here. This verse commands that a person have his sins remitted and receive the Holy Spirit before he is baptized.

The *Book of Mormon* teaches exactly the opposite: "For the gate by which ye should enter is repentance and baptism by water; and then cometh a remission of your sins by fire and by the Holy Ghost" (2 Nephi 31:17). In Mosiah 18:14, Alma is baptized and then receives the Spirit. In 3 Nephi 12:2, remission of sins follows baptism.[14] The materials recently in use by Mormon missionaries also follow this view: "When we are baptized . . . the Lord promises that all our sins will be forgiven, and that he will send his spirit to guide and counsel us."[15]

If the *Doctrine and Covenants* ordering of events is authoritative, then those who are baptized by Mormon missionaries and taught that they must be baptized in order to have the Holy Spirit and forgiveness of sins are being taught false doctrine. If they have been baptized under this misconception, then their baptism is not valid because they have not met the prerequisites for baptism. This serious contradiction is damaging to the Mormon claim that both of these books are divinely inspired.

2. Although the Mormon Church today officially opposes plural marriage, the contradiction on the subject between the *Doctrine and Covenants* and the *Book of Mormon* still remains. *Doctrine and Covenants* 132:4 declares plural marriage to be "a new and an everlasting covenant," which even brings damnation on those who do not accept it. This revelation also explains how Abraham, Isaac, Jacob, Moses and David were justified in having many wives and concubines (*Doctrine and Covenants* 132:29-39). Verses 61-62 of the same chapter describe how this doctrine is to be implemented: A man may take as many wives as he wishes as long as each one is a virgin and is not espoused to another man.

Several passages in the *Book of Mormon* conflict with this revelation. Ether 10:5 says, "And it came to pass that Riplakish did not do that which was right in the sight of the Lord, for he did have many wives and concubines." And Jacob 2:23-24 reads, "They seek to excuse themselves in committing whoredoms, because of the things which were written concerning David, and Solomon his son. Behold, David and Solomon truly had many wives and concubines, which thing was abominable before me, saith the Lord." Another verse (Jacob 3:5) commands that a man have only one wife and no concubines. If both the *Doctrine and Covenants* and the *Book of Mormon* are divinely inspired, then the Mormon god, it seems, has a hard time deciding whether polygamy is good or evil, whether he should command or condemn it.

These are only two of several contradictions between the *Doctrine and Covenants* and the *Book of Mormon,* but they should cause even the most devoted Mormon to doubt that the scriptures he believes have been revealed by God.

The Lectures of Faith

The Lectures of Faith were a series of theological lectures Joseph Smith gave to the elders of the Church in Kirtland, Ohio. They were first printed in the 1835 edition of the *Doctrine and Covenants* and were the reason the word *Doctrine* appeared as part of the title of that work (the *Covenants* was the term for Joseph Smith's revelations). They appeared in all subsequent editions prior to 1921 but they have not appeared in the *Doctrine and Covenants* since. The title page of the 1835 edition makes no distinction in authority between the rest of the revelations and these lectures. The preface implies that both the revelations and the lectures should be accepted as scripture. The last paragraph of the preface says, "We do not present this little volume with any other expectation than that we are to be called to answer to every principle advanced." The preface was signed by Joseph Smith, Oliver Cowdery, Sidney Rigdon and F. G. Williams.

Although the modern Mormon leaders admit that the lectures have been removed, they offer no adequate explanation for their removal, but when the doctrines taught in the lectures are compared to current Mormon doctrine, the reason is evident. The Lectures of Faith propounded things contrary to present Mormon teaching.

Very early in the lectures, Joseph set forth the doctrine of God. In the Lecture Second, verse 2, we read, "We here observe that God is the only supreme governor, and independent being, in whom all fullness and perfection dwells; who is omnipotent, omnipresent, and omnicient [sic]; without beginning of days or end of life." In Lecture Third, verse 15, we discover, "thirdly, that he changes not, neither is there variableness with him; but he is the same from everlasting to everlasting, being the same yesterday today and forever; and that his course is one eternal round, without variation." The current Mormon doctrine of God's being born of a man in another world and progressing to godhood (see p. 17) is not consistent with the God the Lectures Second and Third describe, who has no beginning or end and is changeless.

Lecture Third goes on to state that it is only because God is unchangeable that people can have faith in him. "For without the idea of unchangibleness [sic] in the character of the Deity, doubt would take the place of faith." However, modern Mormons teach that God is continually progressing. Mormon men are planning to become "like God" but never equal to God, for he has a head start and they can never catch him. Can God be eternally unchanging and at the same time constantly changing?

In Lecture Fifth, Joseph considered the attributes of God further. In describing the Father and the Son he said, "The Father being a personage of spirit, glory and power: possessing all perfection and fullness: The Son, who was in the bosom of the Father, *a personage of tabernacle,* made, or fashioned like unto man, or being in the form and likeness of man . . . and is called the Son *because of the flesh*" (emphasis added). According to present-day Mormon teaching, God the Father has a tangible body of flesh and bone while the lecture just quoted says the body of the Son is what makes him different from the Father. God the Father cannot both have flesh and not have flesh at the same time.

Clearly, current Mormon doctrine does not coincide perfectly with the Lectures of Faith, which for nearly one hundred years Mormons accepted as authoritative. Mormon Apostle Mark E. Petersen stated in his book, *As Translated Correctly,* "It seems unthinkable to the honest and devout mind that any man or set of men would deliberately change the text of the word of

God to further their own peculiar purposes."[16] Yet Mormon leaders decided to delete the Lectures of Faith from their sacred books because portions of it contradicted doctrines they wanted to promulgate from the *Doctrine and Covenants.* This action highlights the confusion in the revelations the Mormons claim were given Joseph Smith by God, and points to their human origin.

Chapter 5

THE PEARL
OF GREAT PRICE

The Pearl of Great Price is the shortest of the four standard works of Mormonism. Actually it is a compilation of three different works: (1) the Book of Moses, (2) the Book of Abraham and (3) the Writings of Joseph Smith. The Book of Moses consists of a portion of Joseph Smith's revision of the Bible by divine revelation. It was originally in two parts: (a) Visions of Moses and (b) Writings of Moses. Joseph received the former revelation in June 1830; the latter, in December, 1830. Mormons hold the Book of Abraham to be "a Translation of some Ancient Records, that have fallen into our hands from the Catacombs of Egypt, the Writings of Abraham while he was in Egypt, called the Book of Abraham, written by his own hand, upon Papyrus. Translated from the Papyrus by Joseph Smith."[1] The Writings of Joseph Smith contain Joseph's translation of the twenty-fourth chapter of Matthew from his Bible revision and portions of Joseph's personal history.

The Mormons consider the *Pearl of Great Price* to be as divinely inspired as the Bible. We would expect it, then, to agree with historical reality. But the evidence against the Book of Abraham is by itself so damaging that we can be certain the book is an invention of Joseph Smith's imagination.

Revelation in the Book of Abraham

The Book of Abraham is unique among the extrabiblical scriptures of the Mormons. It alone purports to be a translation of ancient records that are extant for examination. That means it is the only work which came from Joseph Smith that we can study in light of the original papyrus.

How did Joseph Smith acquire the papyrus which he translated and named the Book of Abraham? On July 3, 1835, Michael H. Chandler opened an exhibit in Kirtland, Ohio, which contained four mummies and several papyri covered with hieroglyphics. Joseph, with the help of some of his followers, purchased the mummies and the manuscripts. When Joseph examined the papyri, he declared that one contained the writings of Abraham while he was in Egypt and that another was the work of Joseph, son of Jacob. During the first few months after the purchase, Joseph translated a portion of the papyrus which now constitutes the Book of Abraham 1:1 to 2:18. The remainder he completed in 1842 and the entire work is now printed in the *Pearl of Great Price*.[2]

After Joseph's death, his family was thought to have sold the papyri, to someone who placed it in a Chicago museum.[3] It was thought that the manuscripts were lost in the Chicago fire of 1871 until the following article appeared in the *Deseret News* on November 27, 1967:

New York—A collection of pa[p]yrus manuscripts, long believed to have been destroyed in the Chicago fire of 1871, was presented to the Church of Jesus Christ of Latter-day Saints here Monday by the Metropolitan Museum of Art. . . .

Included in the papyri is a manuscript identified as the original document from which Joseph Smith had copied the drawing which he called "Facsimile No. 1" and published with the Book of Abraham.[4]

Since these manuscripts have come to light, several prominent Egyptologists as well as the Mormon apologist Dr. Hugh Nibley have translated the papyri.[5] When Joseph Smith first wrote down his translation of the Book of Abraham, he placed the Egyptian characters from the papyrus at intervals in the left margin. By comparing the Egyptian letters with those on the papyri rediscovered in 1967, it was easily determined that the fragment labeled "XI. Small 'Sensen' text" was the papyrus Joseph used as the basis for his Book of Abraham translation.[6]

A portion of this translation manuscript is shown in figure 2. Immediately noticeable is the large number of words Joseph Smith used to render each Egyptian character. In this translation manuscript, 1,125 words correspond to 46 Egyptian characters. This is a ratio of 25:1.

Figure 3 shows the rediscovered papyrus with arrows for easy comparison with the handwritten manuscript of Joseph Smith's translation shown in figure 2.[7] Arrow 1 points to the same Egyptian character as it appears in both. It is ⊒ . In its more carefully drawn hieroglyphic form it is written 〰〰 . This character is only one part of the Egyptian word which means "lake" or "pool." To translate this character, Joseph Smith used 76 words and 334 letters. His translation reads:

It was made after the form of a bedstead, such as was had among the Chaldeans, and it stood before the gods of Elkenah, Libnah, Mahmackrah, Korash, and also a god like unto that of Pharaoh, king of Egypt. That you may have an under-

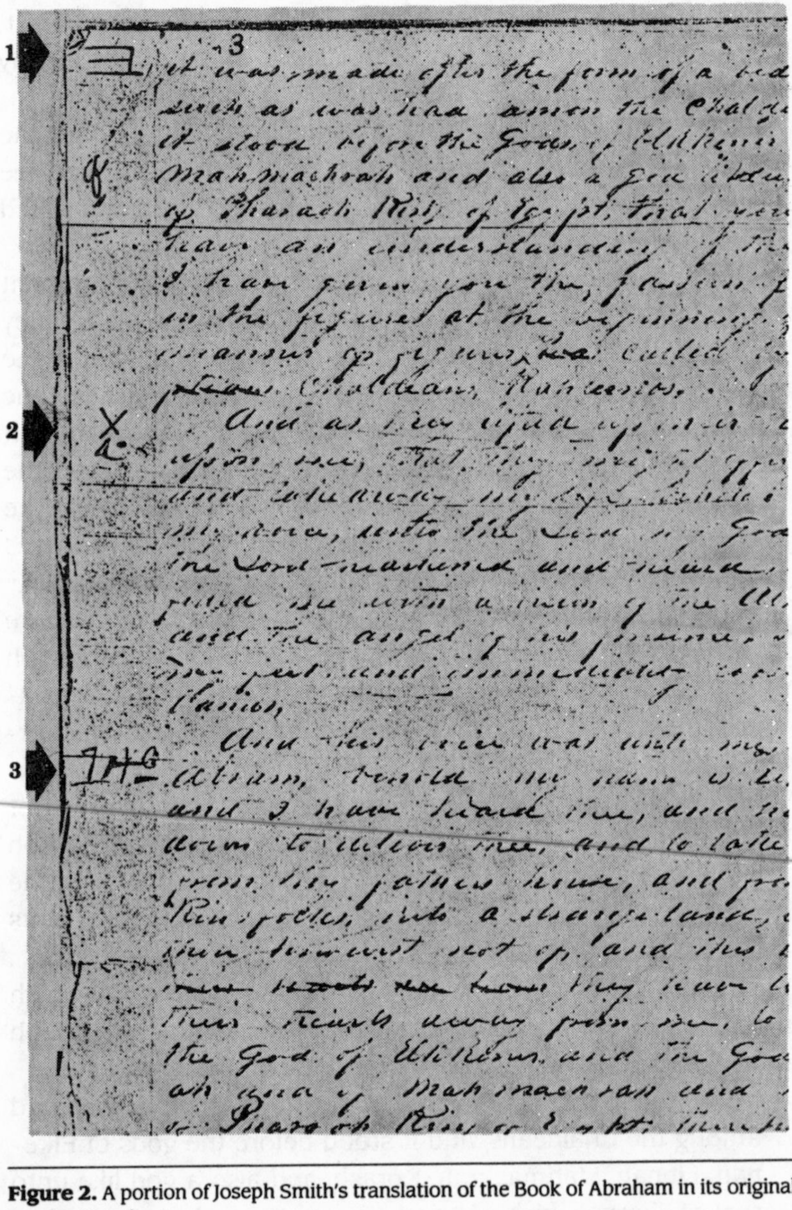

Figure 2. A portion of Joseph Smith's translation of the Book of Abraham in its original handwritten form.

standing of these gods, I have given you the fashion of them in the figures at the beginning, which manner of the figures is called by the Chaldeans Rahleenos, which signifies hiero-glyphics. (Abraham 1:13-14)

To translate the remainder of this single Egyptian word, Joseph used an additional 59 words, making a total of 136 English words from the one Egyptian word. Notice that from this one Egyptian character Joseph's "translation" includes eight differ-ent names of at least two syllables each. There are not enough information channels in this one character to convey such multisyllable names, not to mention the rest of the words of his "translation."

Another Egyptian character on the first line of the Sensen papyrus is 卌 . Dr. Nibley as well as Egyptologist Dr. Klaus

Figure 3. A portion of the "XI. Small 'Sensen' text."

Baer identifies it as the definite article *the,* while Dr. Richard A. Parker renders it by the demonstrative *this.* From this article/demonstrative Joseph Smith translated most of Abraham 1:11: "Now, this priest had offered upon this altar three virgins at one time, who were the daughters of Onitah, one of the royal descent directly from the loins of Ham. These virgins were offered up because of their virtue; they would not bow down to worship gods of wood or of stone, therefore they were killed upon this altar." Thus, 59 words come from the Egyptian equivalent of the English word *the* or *this.*

The phrase ⟨ Egyptian characters ⟩ in the second line of the Sensen text is best translated into English by "born to" or "born of." If the sex of the offspring is known, then it is possible to render it "daughter of" or "son of." In Joseph Smith's translation, three verses (Abraham 1:29-31, with the exception of the last 24 words of verse 31), or 131 words, translate these three Egyptian characters.

Two prominent Egyptologists as well as Dr. Nibley translate the next word in the Sensen text as a proper name. Dr. Klaus Baer renders it Tikhebyt, and Dr. Richard Parker and Dr. Nibley, Taykhebyt. The differences in the spelling can be accounted for by the lack of vocalizations in the Egyptian hieroglyphics. When Joseph Smith came to this name, he divided it into three parts. The first part, ⟨ Egyptian characters ⟩, became, "and I shall endeavor to write some of these things upon this record, for the benefit of my posterity that shall come after me" (Abraham 1:31). The second part, ⟨ Egyptian characters ⟩, became, "Now the Lord God caused the famine to wax sore in the land of Ur, insomuch that Haran, my brother, died; but Terah, my father, yet lived in the land of Ur, of the Chaldees. And it came to pass that I, Abraham, took Sarai to wife, and Nehor, my brother, took Milcah to wife' (Abraham 2:1-2a). (This is a total of 55 words from the center portion of one Egyptian name.) And the third part, ⟨ Egyptian characters ⟩, became "who was the daughter of Haran" (Abraham 2:2b).

The third line of the Sensen text has the word ⳪ ꧂ ꩜ ꩝. Joseph translated Abraham 2:12-13 from three of the four letters of this Egyptian term. This word may be translated either "his heart" (Baer) or "his breast" (Parker and Nibley). It is generally agreed that this spelling was never used prior to 400 B.C., contradicting the claim that it was written by Abraham, who lived approximately 2000 B.C.

We could continue to make comparisons of the Book of Abraham with the Egyptian text, but we have already seen enough to know that Joseph's translation in no way corresponds to the writing on the papyrus. From the 46 characters in the manuscript, Smith produced 1,125 English words, including over 65 proper names. In English, this represents approximately 296 vocables, and this count does not include those of a connecting type that are least audible.

One further point. In language translation, proper names are most often transliterated rather than translated. In Joseph Smith's version, the name Mahmackrah appears three times with seven vocables each time. Shagreel, a proper name with six vocables, occurs once. Elkenah has five vocables and appears five separate times. That makes a total of 52 vocables for those three names alone. Therefore, the 46 characters that Joseph translated cannot even account for the nine occurrences of these three words, much less the remaining 1,073 words.

If the Sensen text Joseph used to produce the Book of Abraham does not really contain the words of Abraham, then what would an accurate translation of the Sensen text be? Dr. Klaus Baer of the prestigious University of Chicago's Oriental Institute translates it this way:

Osiris shall be conveyed into the Great Pool of Khons—and likewise Osiris Hôr, *justified,* born to Tikhebyt, justified—after his arms have been *pla*ced on his heart and the Breathing

Permit (which [Isis] made and has writing on its inside and outside) has been wrapped in royal linen and placed under his left arm near his heart; the rest of his mummy-bandages should be wrapped over it. The man for whom this book has been copied will breathe forever and ever as the bas of the gods do.[8]

The title of the scroll of which this fragment is a part is found in the text of the fragment. It was called the *Book of Breathings*. We know from a similar papyrus in the Louvre which includes the preamble to the *Book of Breathings* that the purpose of the papyrus was to aid the deceased on their journey through the afterlife.

Book of Abraham Facsimiles

When Joseph Smith received the mummies and papyri, several of the papyri had only vignettes or pictures on them. In preparing the Book of Abraham for publication, he had three of these Egyptian vignettes transferred to woodcuts and printed in the text as illustrations of the narration in the Book of Abraham. He called them *Facsimiles 1, 2 and 3.*

We must keep in mind that the Small Sensen text, which we have just examined, was found with the mummies. From the Egyptologists' translation of it, we know that the entire *Book of Breathings* was to be placed with a corpse for protection and guidance in the afterlife. Klaus Baer concluded after careful study that the fragments—the Small Sensen text, the Larger Sensen text and the fragment Joseph Smith identified as the original of Facsimile 1—were all part of the same scroll.[9] This is significant for our study, because if these pieces were all part of the same scroll, Facsimile 1 must also belong to the *Book of Breathings*. When compared to the copy of the *Book of Breathings* in the British Museum, it seems quite probable that the picture Joseph called Facsimile 3 was also attached to the same scroll by a piece of the papyrus that is now missing.[10]

Scholars have long considered Facsimile 2 in the Book of Abraham to be a hypocephalus, a disk that was placed under the head of a mummy.[11] Since the hypocephalus is not considered a part of the *Book of Breathings* scroll, we shall consider it separately, and then return to Facsimiles 1 and 3.

Facsimile 2, as it appears in the Book of Abraham, has been found by prominent Egyptologists to contain many inaccuracies and adulterations. For example, a line of hieroglyphics that runs along the rim of this disk-shaped hypocephalus is interrupted by hieratic writing. This in itself is unusual, to say the least, and even more surprising is that the hieratic writing has been inserted upside down.[12]

For some time it was not known where the hieratic letters came from. After the papyri became available in 1967, the Tanners compared the hieratic letters with the writing on the Small Sensen text and found that in several places groups of letters matched perfectly[13] (see figure 4). They could see no reason, though, for these insertions until they were able to obtain copies of what the Mormon Church has called *Joseph Smith's Egyptian Papers*. On one sheet Joseph Smith had copied the original hypocephalus. The original, it turns out, was incomplete, indicating that the papyrus had been damaged before Joseph Smith purchased it. Comparing it with the woodcut of the same hypocephalus in the Book of Abraham, the Tanners found that the letters and pictures the Egyptologists had considered adulterations were missing.[14]

When Joseph Smith placed Facsimile 2 in the Book of Abraham, he labeled various parts of it and included a translation of several of these parts. Some of the parts he labeled (1) "Ought not to be revealed at this present time"; (2) "If the world can find out these numbers, so let it be"; and (3) "will be given in the own due time of the Lord." It is obvious that Joseph Smith

A FACSIMILE FROM THE BOOK OF ABRAHAM

No. 2

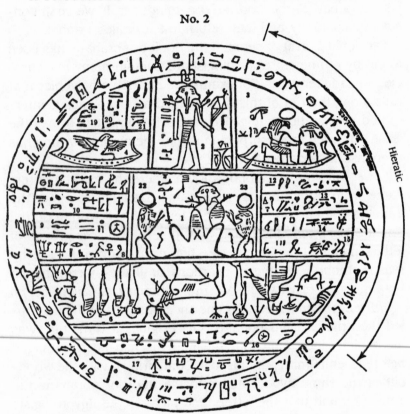

Figure 4. Facsimile 2, Hypocephalus

had no idea what these parts of the hypocephalus meant.[15] From the Mormon Scholar Michael Rhodes's translation and comments on Facsimile 2, it is clear that parts Joseph *did* identify likewise were equally unknown to him.[16]

In Joseph Smith's explanation of this hypocephalus, he used proper names like Abraham, Adam, Seth, Noah, Melchizedek and Kolob. Rhodes's translation has no names that remotely resemble them.[17] It is hard to reach any other conclusion than that Joseph Smith's explanations were products of his creative imagination.

Facsimiles 1 and 3, as previously mentioned, are undoubtedly part of the same scroll. Facsimile 1, according to Joseph Smith, is a drawing of the priest of Elkenah attempting to offer Abraham as a sacrifice to the gods Elkenah, Libnah, Mahmackrah, Korash and Pharaoh.[18] When Dr. Richard A. Parker examined the original vignette of Facsimile 1, he made these observations:

> This is a well-known scene from the Osiris mysteries, with Anubis, the jackal-headed god, on the left ministering to the dead Osiris on the bier. The pencilled (?) restoration is incorrect. Anubis should be jackal-headed. The left arm of Osiris is in reality lying at his side under him. The apparent upper hand is part of the wing of a second bird which is hovering over the erect phallus of Osiris (now broken away). The second bird is Isis and she is magically impregnated by the dead Osiris and then later gives birth to Horus who avenges his father and takes over his inheritance. The complete bird represents Nephthys, sister to Osiris and Isis. Beneath the bier are the four canopic jars with heads representative of tthe four sons of Horus, human-headed Imseti, baboon-headed Hapy, jackal-headed Duamutef and falcon-headed Kebehsenuf. The hieroglyphs refer to burial, etc.[19]

Parker's observations are completely at variance with the interpretation the Book of Abraham gives.

The papyrus fragment of this scene has several items that are not shown on the copy in the Book of Abraham (see figures 5 and 6). It has several rows of Egyptian characters on the sides and a small portion of what appears to have been a row of characters across the top. In these characters are several names. Two of them are Amon–Re and Osiris. These same names are found on other copies of the *Book of Breathings*. Another name that appears on this facsimile is the name for the falcon–god Horus, which most Egyptologists render Hor. This name also appears on both of the Sensen fragments and Facsimile 3.[20] Although Hor appears on three of the four fragments, it is not found anywhere in Joseph Smith's work, nor do the names Amon–Re or Osiris appear in his translation.

Facsimile 3 is a drawing with six figures, five standing and one seated (see figure 7). In his explanation of this drawing, Joseph Smith names and numbers each of these figures. Figure 1 is Abraham, 2 is Pharaoh, 3 signifies Abraham in Egypt, 4 is the Prince of Pharaoh, 5 is Shulem and 6 is Olimlah the slave.[21] Klaus Baer was able to translate most of the hieroglyphics on Facsimile 3. The results yield a totally different identification. Figure 1 is the god Osiris, 2 is the goddess Isis, 3 is an offering-stand, 4 is the goddess Maat, 5 is Hor and 6 is the god Anubis.

Joseph Smith's most ludicrous blunder was in identifying the two goddesses in female clothing as Pharaoh and his son. Baer's interpretation is based on the Egyptian identifications written above each figure's head as well as the well–known symbolism used in Egyptian funeral paintings. He summarizes his findings in these words.

"Facsimile No. 3" shows a man (5), his hand raised in adoration and a cone of perfumed grease and a lotus flower on his head (ancient Egyptian festival attire), being introduced by Maat (4), the goddess of justice, and Anubis (6), the guide of the dead, into the presence of Osiris (1), enthroned as king of the Netherworld. Behind Osiris stands Isis (2), and in front of him is an offering-stand (3) with a jug and some flowers on it. Over the whole scene is a canopy with stars painted on it to represent the sky.

The scene comes from a mortuary papyrus. . . . It is a summary in one illustration of what the *Breathing Permit* promised: The deceased, after successfully undergoing the judgment, is welcomed into the presence of Osiris.[22]

Joseph Smith's explanation is far from accurate. All three of the facsimiles have a significance that in no way relates to the meaning he poured into them.[23]

Since the papyri were first rediscovered in 1967, Mormon writers have made various attempts to justify Joseph Smith's erroneous identifications and his fictitious translation. It has been suggested, for example, that the Egyptian text was a "super-cryptogram" to which Joseph was given the key by direct revelation; and again, that it was a memory device to which the Book of Abraham was tied, and only the Prophet was given the "translation."[24] However, most of these attempts have now been abandoned, and Mormons tend to follow the 1975 assertions of Dr. Hugh Nibley. He claims that the text from which Joseph Smith made his translation was cut off from the papyrus bearing the vignette, which Joseph reproduced as Facsimile 1, and is still lost.[25]

Such wishful thinking by Nibley will not hold up in the light of the evidence itself. For example, Facsimile 1 was identified by Joseph as a part of the Book of Abraham and clearly belongs with the Sensen texts numbers XI and X that adjoin the vignette to the *left.*

This has been indisputably established by Klaus Baer, not only by his personal examination of the papyri, but also by his translation of both of the Sensen texts as well as of the hier-

Figure 5. Vignette from a Roman era funeral papyrus acquired by Joseph Smith, Jr., in 1835. It is a vignette or illustration that accompanied a "Breathing Permit" which Egyptians thought would enable the corpse to live and breathe again in the next life. The hieroglyphic character encircled indicates that the deceased was named Hor or Horus. Other hieroglyphics indicate that his father was a priest named Osorwer and his mother was Tikhebyt.

Figure 6. Facsimile 1. In his periodical, *Times and Seasons,* Joseph Smith falsely identified the same Egyptian vignette as a facsimile from the Book of Abraham, showing that he mistakenly thought this pagan "Breathing Permit" was actually the work of the patriarch Abraham some two thousand years earlier.

TIMES AND SEASONS.

"Truth will prevail."

Vol. III No. 9.]   CITY OF NAUVOO, ILL. MARCH, 1, 1842.   [Whole No. 45.

A FACSIMILE FROM THE BOOK OF ABRAHAM.
NO. 1.

Figure 7. This is a copy of Facsimile No. 3 as printed in the *Times and Seasons,* issue of May 16, 1842, and represented to be from the "Book of Abraham." Figure No. 5 (second from the right) is the deceased person, identified as Horus or Hor in the characters above his hand and in the prayer at the bottom of the picture. The presence of this name ties this vignette to the vignette from which Smith derived his Facsimile 1, as well as with the papyrus fragment known as the little Sensen XI. Thus it demonstrates that Joseph Smith regarded the Breathing Permit of Hor as the Book Abraham had written. Notice that in Joseph Smith's identification Pharaoh and his son are both wearing women's clothes. In the drawing above Joseph Smith's identifications are listed above the figures while those of professional Egyptologists are listed below the figures.

oglyphic characters that flank the vignette that Smith reproduced as Facsimile 1.[26] These characters definitely identify by
name the person for whom the papyrus vignette and also the
adjoining Sensen texts were intended, "Hôr, son of the priest
Osorwêr and the lady Tikhebyt."[27]

That Joseph regarded the Sensen No. XI papyrus as the text
from which he thought he was getting his Book of Abraham
is evident from the manuscripts containing his "translation" in
which single symbols from Sensen No. XI are written in a column on the left of the page headed "[Ch]aracter," and Book of
Abraham segments are written on the right in a broad column
headed "Translation . . ." Mormon scholar Edward H. Ashment,
a doctoral candidate in Egyptian from the University of Chicago's Oriental Institute, has carefully examined these translation
manuscripts and established beyond reasonable dispute that
Joseph regarded the Breathing Permit of Hôr as the Book of
Abraham. At a Sunstone lecture in 1984 he concluded from his
study of the evidence that "it should now be clear that the
'Egyptian original' of the Book of Abraham is not lost—in spite
of assertions to the contrary."[28] He acknowledged that the rec-
ognition that we have the Egyptian text from which Joseph
claimed to derive his Book of Abraham translation still leaves
Mormons with an unresolved conflict between their prophet
and recognized Egyptian scholars. However, he concluded that
"there is no factual basis to the rationalizations which have
been devised to explain away the dissonances caused to the
Book of Abraham—by the Joseph Smith papyri."[29]

Only those who wish to preserve the fantasy that Joseph
Smith was given the ability to translate the Book of Abraham
still vainly try to defend his work. After the rediscovered papyri
appeared, Thomas Stuart Ferguson hired two Egyptologists to
translate the published Egyptian text independently. His conclusion is the only reasonable position that can be reached in

the light of all the clear evidence:

Joseph Smith announced, in print *(History of the Church,* Vol. 11, p. 236) that "one of the rolls contained the writings of Abraham, another the writings of Joseph of Egypt . . ." Since 4 scholars, who have established that they can read Egyptian, say that the manuscripts deal with neither Abraham nor Joseph—and since the 4 reputable men tell us exactly what the manuscripts do say—I must conclude that Joseph Smith had not the remotest skill in things Egyptian-hieroglyphics. To my surprise, one of the highest officials in the Mormon church agreed with that conclusion when I made that very statement to him on Dec. 4, 1970—privately in one-to-one [c]onversation.[30]

Hopefully, both Mormons and Christians who take the time to investigate the matter will reach the same irresistible conclusion.

Chapter 6

WITNESSING
TO MORMONS

Mormonism is not Christian. And the documents out of which its unorthodox doctrines come are not divinely inspired. Being sure of this ourselves, how can we persuade those who are not convinced? How can we use the information we have to lead Mormons to a true knowledge of Christ?

This is not an easy subject to approach. Since each Mormon is an individual with unique needs and at a unique stage of doubting or accepting Mormonism, we cannot develop a step-by-step approach that will work with all Mormons at all times. If we are witnessing to a Mormon bishop, our approach will necessarily be different from the way we deal with a recent Mormon convert. We can, however, lay down some general principles to adapt to specific situations.

The New Testament gives us the essential principles in 2

Timothy 2:24–26. In this passage the apostle Paul is telling Timothy how to interact with those who oppose him:

> And the Lord's bond-servant must not be quarrelsome, but be kind to all, able to teach, patient when wronged, with gentleness correcting those who are in opposition, if perhaps God may grant them repentance leading to the knowledge of the truth, and they may come to their senses *and escape* from the snare of the devil, having been held captive by him to do his will.

Paul addresses these instructions to the Lord's *bond-servant.* The Greek word is the common term for a slave. When applied to a relation between God and a human being, it refers to a person whom God owns body and soul. Paul uses it here and in other passages to mean any follower of Christ. All Christians, then, should heed these principles in their witnessing.

The Lord's bond-servant must not be quarrelsome. To be *quarrelsome* means "to do verbal battle." We are not to engage in verbal warfare with those to whom we witness. Enemies, not friends, are made when an encounter turns into an argument. To maintain the long-term friendship with a Mormon that is necessary for a fruitful witness, we cannot sacrifice friendship to make a point.

Friendship is of the utmost importance in witnessing to most Mormons. For one thing, as we get to know a person more intimately, we are better able to discern which information, of all the information we could give him, he most needs to hear. I once met a man who had been a Christian minister for nearly twenty-five years before becoming a Mormon. He revealed that there were several Christian doctrines he would never be able to give up and that the Mormon Church accepted these doctrines. One of them was the virgin birth. He had not learned that the Mormons believe God the Father had physical relations with Mary. This was, therefore, a good place to start in trying to win him back to Christianity. Planting one doubt about Mormon doctrine or the Mormon scriptures may raise a harvest of further questioning.

Being *kind,* rather than argumentative, does not rule out being a bold witness for the Lord; instead, it implies being tactful, saying the right thing in the right way at the right time. We cannot compromise the truth, but it does no good to pistol-whip a Mormon with the Bible. John L. Smith, a student of Mormonism for more than twenty-five years, makes a relevant comment about the many occurrences of the word *boldness* in Acts:

> The words translated "boldly and boldness" here came from words that mean "outspoken, frankness, bluntness, and by implication, assurance. To be frank in utterance or confident in spirit and demeanor."
>
> A witness to Mormons must be bold. The Mormon is bold—often almost to the point of arrogance—and any successful witness to him must be courageous and forward. Any hesitation on the part of the witness is interpreted by the Mormon as weakness and error. He is used to seeing non-Mormons who are timid and unsure of themselves. He sees the Mormon self-assuredness as an indication of his being "right." Therefore, the fearful, timid, flinching, fainthearted witness has already almost defeated his effort by his lack of "boldness."[1]

Smith adds that he is not advocating either harshness or arrogance as New Testament *boldness.*

The Lord's bond-servant must also be *able to teach.* A witness who does not know his material will not easily succeed. In talking with a Mormon, we must know more than just the Bible. The Bible is essential and should take the foremost position, but we must know the Mormon outlook as well.

Paul showed by his approach in Acts 17:16–34 that he understood Stoic and Epicurean philosophy. He did not learn these Greek world views in his Bible. Yet it was because he understood how the pagan mind worked that he was able to see results from his bold encounter with the Court of the Areopagus. Paul had to pave the way for their reception of God's truth by showing these philosophers that their ideas were inadequate. As a result of Paul's witness "some men joined him and believed, among whom also was Dionysius the Areopagite and a woman named Damaris and others with them" (Acts 17:34).

If we are gentle yet bold, and able to teach, God may perhaps use our words to convince people of the truth.

Where Should You Start?

If you are new at witnessing to Mormons, you should not try to witness to Mormon missionaries. There are several reasons for this. One is that Mormon missionaries usually work in pairs, which gives them an advantage in dealing with a single Christian. Another is that Mormon missionaries are told they should not spend time with anyone they do not think they can convert. If you resist their doctrine, they probably will not return for a second conversation. If you succeed in raising a question that causes them to check with their superiors, they will in all likelihood be transferred to a new area.

A person with enough experience can accomplish with Mormon missionaries what Charles Crane, a man who has witnessed to Mormons for twenty-five years, calls "knocking the polish off their testimony." By this, Crane means getting a Mormon to doubt Mormonism enough that he will have a hard time telling potential converts he "knows" the *Book of Mormon* and the Mormon Church are true. This will greatly decrease his effectiveness in leading people into Mormonism.

The best place for you to start is probably with a Mormon

friend or relative with whom you are comfortable and whom you know well. This enables you to know how to approach the person and how far you can go without starting an argument and losing a friend.

The plan that seems most effective in talking with Mormons involves these three steps: (1) showing that the Bible is trustworthy, (2) showing that the *Book of Mormon,* the *Doctrine and Covenants* and the *Pearl of Great Price* are not God's Word, and (3) getting a Mormon to realize that his faith in the *Book of Mormon* and Mormonism is purely subjective. Let us examine each of these three steps more closely.

As we discussed in chapter one, Mormons believe the Bible is unreliable because the Bible manuscripts have been almost hopelessly corrupted in transmission. You must, therefore, support the Bible's integrity before you use any verses from it. If you fail to do this, any verse you quote that contradicts Mormon doctrine will simply be written off as one of those places at which the Bible cannot be trusted.

Many Mormons have discovered the errors of Mormonism without the aid of a Christian. This was the case with the founder of the New World Archeological Society, Thomas Stuart Ferguson, who came to doubt Mormonism because of the evidence against it. But Ferguson, like many Mormons who lose faith in Mormonism, also abandoned the Bible! Mormons already distrust the Bible. If you do not build up their confidence in it, you may turn them against Christianity as well as Mormonism.

Evidence for the trustworthiness of the Bible is plentiful. In the following several paragraphs we will survey the kind of information you can share with a Mormon.

Most of the important evidence for the accurate transmission of the Old Testament comes from the Dead Sea Scrolls. The first pieces were discovered in 1946 when a shepherd boy threw a rock into a cave near the Dead Sea and heard a jar break. This led to a series of excavations that uncovered one of the richest biblical manuscript finds ever.

The Dead Sea Scrolls contain portions of every Old Testament book except Esther. Until the discovery of these manuscripts, the oldest Old Testament manuscript in existence dated from around A.D. 900. The Dead Sea Scrolls were produced between 200 B.C. and A.D. 68. That means the Dead Sea Scrolls are from 900 to 1,100 years older than the oldest previously existing manuscript. The Mormons' claim that the Bible (in this case the Old Testament) was changed and corrupted by the Catholic Church, can now be tested.

To illustrate the *accuracy* of the transmission of the Hebrew Old Testament, consider how little the Masoretic text of Isaiah 53 (produced in A.D. 916 and used in making most English translations including the King James Version) differs from Isaiah 53 in a portion of the Dead Sea Scrolls (dated 125 B.C.):

Of the 166 words in Isaiah 53, there are only seventeen letters in question. Ten of these letters are simply a matter of spelling, which does not affect the sense. Four more letters are minor stylistic changes, such as conjunctions. The remaining three letters comprise the word "light," which is added in verse 11, and does not affect the meaning greatly. . . . Thus, in one chapter of 166 words, there is only one word (three letters) in question after a thousand years of transmission—and this word does not significantly change the meaning of the passage.[2]

Gleason Archer states that the Isaiah scroll is word-for-word identical with our standard Hebrew Old Testament in over ninety-five per cent of the text. He attributes the five per cent variation to obvious slips of the pen and variations in spelling.[3]

The accuracy of the transmission of the Old Testament text can be accounted for by the strict regulations under which

Jewish scribes worked. Samuel Davidson describes how the Talmudist went about making a copy of the Old Testament text. The minute regulations were as follows:

(1) A synagogue roll must be written on the skins of clean animals, (2) prepared for the particular use of the synagogue by a Jew. (3) These must be fastened together with strings taken from clean animals. (4) Every skin must contain a certain number of columns, equal throughout the entire codex. (5) The length of each column must not extend over less than 48 or more than 60 lines; and the breadth must consist of thirty letters. (6) The whole copy must be first-lined; and if three words be written without a line, it is worthless. (7) The ink should be black, neither red, green, nor any other colour, and be prepared according to a definite recipe. (8) An authentic copy must be the exemplar, from which the transcriber ought not in the least deviate. (9) No word or letter, not even a yod, must be written from memory, the scribe not having looked at the codex before him. . . . (10) Between every consonant the space of a hair or thread must intervene. (11) Between every new parashah, or section, the breadth of nine consonants; (12) between every book, three lines. (13) The fifth book of Moses must terminate exactly with a line; but the rest need not do so. (14) Besides this, the copyist must sit in full Jewish dress, (15) wash his whole body, (16) not begin to write the name of God with a pen newly dipped in ink, (17) and should a king address him while writing that name he must take no notice of him.[4]

Rolls that did not measure up to the standards were destroyed. These rigid copying standards were followed from about the New Testament period onward and account for the great degree of accuracy with which our Old Testament text was copied over the centuries.

Thus the Old Testament we have today is for all practical

purposes identical to the texts used before Jesus' time. This is fatal to the Mormon claim that the Catholic Church has made it impossible for us to have a correct Bible. Even if we had found significant doctrinal differences between the Dead Sea Scrolls and our Old Testament, we would now have the older manuscripts with which to correct our current text.

There is an even greater abundance of manuscript evidence for the accuracy of the transmission of the New Testament. According to Bruce Metzger, we now have nearly five thousand manuscripts that contain all or part of the New Testament. They date from approximately A.D. 130 to A.D. 1200. Considering that these manuscripts were written in a span of over a thousand years by thousands of different scribes all over the world, we would expect a large number of variations in the readings. There are, in fact, in excess of 150,000 textual variants. Yet, as Geisler and Nix point out, "There is an ambiguity in saying there are some 200,000 variants in the existing manuscripts of the New Testament, since they represent only 10,000 places in the New Testament. If one single word is misspelled in 3,000 different manuscripts, this is counted as 3,000 variants or readings."[5]

F. F. Bruce, with keen insight into the discipline of textual criticism, concludes, "When we have documents like our New Testament writings copied and recopied thousands of times, the scope for copyists' errors is so enormously increased that it is surprising there are no more than there actually are. Fortunately, if the great number of MSS increases the number of scribal errors, it increases proportionately the means of correcting such errors, so that the margin of doubt left in the process of recovering the exact original wording is not so large as might be feared; it is in truth remarkably small."[6]

B. F. Westcott and F. J. A. Hort, famous for their 1881 critical edition of the Greek New Testament, note that "if comparative trivialities, such as changes of order, the insertion or omission of the article with proper names, and the like, are set aside, the words in our opinion still subject to doubt can hardly amount to more than a thousandth part of the whole New Testament.[7] It should also be remembered that we know exactly where significant variants occur and what words or phrases are involved in these variations.

Several of the best and most complete manuscripts have a rather early date; two of them—the Codex Vaticanus and the Codex Sinaiticus—are as early as A.D. 350. Also important is the Chester Beatty Papyri, consisting of parts of eleven codices, three of which contain most of the New Testament writings. These codices have been assigned dates ranging from A.D. 250 to 350. The John Rylands Papyrus is probably the oldest New Testament manuscript yet found. It contains portions of John 18:31–33, 37–38. It is dated about A.D. 130. Also supporting our present Gospel of John is the Bodmer II Papyrus. It has the first fourteen chapters of John and much of the remaining seven chapters and is dated about A.D. 200, little more than one hundred years after the original composition.[8]

With these thousands of manuscripts with hundreds of thousands of variations, it is striking that no important doctrinal issues are at stake in any of the disputed readings. Philip Schaff maintains that not one of the variations alters "an article of faith or a precept of duty which is not abundantly sustained by other and undoubted passages, or by the whole tenor of Scripture teaching."[9]

We must agree therefore with the late Sir Frederic Kenyon:
The interval then between the dates of the original composition and the earliest extant evidence becomes so small as to be in fact negligible, and the last foundation for any doubt that the Scriptures have come down to us substantially as they were written has now been removed. Both the *authen-*

ticity and the *general integrity* of the books of the New Testament may be regarded as finally established.[10]
Joseph Smith and other early Mormon leaders did not have sufficient evidence to make the claims they made about the Bible. Modern scholarship has established the reliability of the Old and New Testament manuscript traditions beyond question.

Creating Doubt

You must use evidence like this to remove a Mormon's doubt about the trustworthiness of the Bible and then replace that doubt with doubt in the extrabiblical documents the Mormons regard as sacred. Remember that in raising doubt you are not trying to destroy the Mormon's personal faith. Rather you are seeking to transfer his faith from the false foundation of Mormonism to the true foundation of the Bible. Therefore, creating doubt plays a large part in an effective witness to a Mormon. You must be in continual prayer that God's Spirit will lead you to raise the right questions. Once a Mormon has begun to doubt, evidence that never carried any weight before suddenly begins to make sense. You can then share additional facts as fast as the person can receive them without becoming overwhelmed or angry with you.

One way to raise doubt about whether the *Book of Mormon* is the Word of God is to point out serious differences between its teachings and Mormon doctrine. As we have learned, the *Book of Mormon* does not contain basic Mormon doctrine. As a matter of fact, the *Book of Mormon* often contradicts it and teaches orthodox Christian positions.

An important example of this is the doctrine of God. Mormons believe in a God that has a body of flesh and bone, who lives in heaven (the First Estate) with his wives, who is procreating spirit-children, who is completely separate and distinct from Jesus, who is perhaps just one of thousands of gods that exist in the universe, who is literally the father of Jesus both in spirit and the flesh, and who has progressed from being a man to being a God and will continue to progress through eternity. These teachings are totally absent from the *Book of Mormon*. Most Mormons are not aware of this. On the contrary, the *Book of Mormon* teaches the Christian doctrine of God, as these verses show:

(1) Only one God: Alma 11:21-22, 28-31; 3 Nephi 11:27, 36; 2 Nephi 11:7; 2 Nephi 31:21; Mosiah 15:1-5; Mosiah 16:15; (2) God the Father and Son have been God eternally: Alma 11:38-39, 44; 2 Nephi 26:12; (3) God is unchanging: Mormon 9:9-11; Moroni 7:22; Moroni 8:18; (4) God is a Spirit: Alma 18:24-28; Alma 22:9-11; 31:15.

If you are serious about witnessing to Mormons, you should study each of these verses in its context. With the aid of a concordance to the *Book of Mormon*, you can add to this list or produce a similar list on other doctrines. Most copies of the *Book of Mormon* contain a concordance and cross-reference system. You may find the list in Appendix B helpful here.

A good way to present these verses is to ask a Mormon what he believes about God. Get him to say it aloud. Many times a Mormon will be reluctant to do this because he knows his beliefs about God will be repulsive to a Christian. But prod him if necessary, because it is important that he state his beliefs.

If he does not object, jot down his doctrine of God as he gives it. When his ideas are out in the open, ask him to show you some verses in the *Book of Mormon* that support them. He will hunt in vain—for there are none. (As far as I know, he could appeal to only one chapter in the *Book of Mormon*, Ether 3. Several times this section mentions the finger of God. But this anthropomorphism does not prove that God has a physical body any more than Psalm 91:4 [KJV], "He shall cover thee with his feathers, and under his wings shalt thou trust," proves that God is a cosmic chicken.)

Then use the verses listed above to show that the *Book of Mormon* actually teaches the Christian doctrine of God. You might say something like this, "I know that you accept the *Book of Mormon* as the Word of God, but I do not. I do believe, though, that it contains some true statements about God. If I can show you that the *Book of Mormon* teaches my doctrine of God, and not yours, will you accept that doctrine?" While doing this, make use of what you wrote down as the Mormon was explaining his concept of God, refuting these ideas point by point.

Then, by comparing the beliefs about God which the Mormon has listed with what is said in the verses listed on page 107, show that the *Book of Mormon* actually teaches a doctrine of God which is different from the Mormon doctrine.

The first verses in the list are powerful when taken in context. In Alma 11:21-29 is a conversation between Amulek, a prophet of God, and Zeezrom, a "man who was expert in the devices of the devil, that he might destroy that which was good." Zeezrom, hoping to trick Amulek into betraying God, begins to question him: "Will ye answer the questions which I shall put unto you?" And Amulek said unto him: "Yea, if it be according to the Spirit of the Lord, which is in me; for I shall say nothing which is contrary to the Spirit of the Lord." Zeezrom asks Amulek pointblank, "Is there more than one God?" And Amulek answers, "No."

Point out to your friend that he has just told you there are many gods in the universe and that Jesus and the Father are separate and distinct gods. How can he square that belief with this statement by a prophet of God? Some Mormons will answer, "What the prophet meant was that there is only one God with whom we have anything to do." To which you can respond, "If that is what he meant, why isn't that what he said?" Also, Mormons do not really believe this answer, for they think that Jesus and the Father are two completely separate gods and that we have something to do with both of them. Press the issue gently, "Which do you accept, the *Book of Mormon* or Mormon doctrine? You cannot believe both."

Another key verse is 2 Nephi 31:21: "And now, behold, this is the doctrine of Christ, and the only and true doctrine of the Father, and of the Son, and of the Holy Ghost, which is one God, without end." You need to emphasize two things in this verse. First, it purports to teach "the only true doctrine" about the person of God. Second, it teaches the essential oneness of the three persons of the Godhead.

The standard Mormon objection is that this verse is pointing to the fact that they are one in purpose. Again, if this is what the author meant, why isn't it what the author said? In fact, not one verse in the *Book of Mormon* says they are only one in purpose.

Eternal progression, the concept that God is a man who has progressed to godhood and that any man today can also achieve godhood, is an important Mormon idea about God that is absent from and even opposed by the *Book of Mormon.*[11] Consider Mormon 9:9–10, for example: "For do we not read that God is the same yesterday, today, and forever, and in him there is no variableness neither shadow of changing? And now if ye have imagined up unto yourselves a god who doth vary, and in whom there is shadow of changing, then have ye imagined up unto yourselves a god who is not a God of miracles."[12] In the same context, Mormon 9:19 asserts, "And behold, I say unto you he changeth not; if so he would cease to be God." Moroni 8:18 further widens the gap between Mormon doctrine and the *Book of Mormon:* "For I know that God is not a partial God, neither a changeable being; but is unchangeable from all eternity to all eternity." Joseph Smith shortly before his death expressly contradicted this *Book of Mormon* teaching. He stated, "We have imagined and supposed that God was God from all eternity. I will refute that idea."[13]

You cannot stress this contradiction enough. Present Mormon doctrine teaches that God has changed and will continue to change forever according to the law of eternal progression, while the *Book of Mormon* teaches that God has been the same for all eternity past and will be the same for all eternity to come. Mormons must give up either Mormon doctrine, or the *Book of Mormon,* or both.[14]

Most Mormons will want to use the *Doctrine and Covenants* when they can find no ready help in the *Book of Mormon.* In such a case, you should refer the Mormon to *Doctrine and Covenants* 18:1-5, which claims that the *Book of Mormon* contains "all things written concerning the foundation of my church, my gospel, and my rock." The doctrine of God would seem to be a foundation doctrine and crucial to understanding the gospel; therefore, it should be found in the *Book of Mormon.*

Once your Mormon friend has begun to see the contradictions between Mormon doctrine and the *Book of Mormon,* you can share more of the material we have already discussed in this book. The changes in the *Book of Commandments* are a good topic to turn to next. Realizing a few things about the changes will help you in presenting them.

One of the most important verses to use is *Book of Commandments* 1:7 and the duplicate statement in *Doctrine and Covenants* 1:37-39. You must emphasize that these verses assert that *Book of Commandments* and *Doctrine and Covenants* are God's Word and will stand forever. Whenever you point out a change in one of the revelations, you should remind your hearer about these verses to show that these books do not measure up to their own claims.

The three most important changes to share are those between *Book of Commandments* 4:2 and *Doctrine and Covenants* 5:4; *Book of Commandments* 6 and *Doctrine and Covenants* 7; and *Book of Commandments* 15:1-4 and *Doctrine and Covenants* 18:1-5.

The first change undercuts the inspiration of all books written by Joseph Smith except the *Book of Mormon.* Actually, two of the three extrabiblical scriptures the Mormons claim are God's Word stand or fall with this change. The second change concerns the reliability of the *Book of Commandments,* the *Doctrine and Covenants* and the *Book of Mormon.* If Joseph could not even translate a three-verse passage correctly with the Urim and Thummim, how can we trust the nearly six hundred pages of the *Book of Mormon* that were translated in the same way? The third change is important because it deals with the content of the *Book of Mormon.* Does the *Book of Mormon* contain all things or not? When using this change be sure to use the entire context or the Mormon will say the "things written" are all the extrabiblical Mormon scriptures.

Ask your Mormon friend, "If these revelations are God's Word as you claim, why haven't they remained unchanged as *Book of Commandments* 1:7 and *Doctrine and Covenants* 1:37-39 claimed they would?" Press home the importance of these three changes; all of Mormonism stands or falls on them. (To help the serious student study changes not discussed in this book and to facilitate comparing verses in the *Book of Commandments* and the *Doctrine and Covenants,* a chart showing the parallel chapters in each is included in Appendix C.)

The third important element of a witness to a Mormon is showing him that his faith in the *Book of Mormon* and Mormonism is subjective. In the front of most of the missionary editions of the *Book of Mormon* is printed Moroni 10:4-5, which reads, "And when ye shall receive these things, I would exhort you that ye would ask God, the Eternal Father, in the name of Christ, if these things are not true; and if ye shall ask with a sincere heart, with real intent, having faith in Christ, he will manifest the truth of it unto you, by the power of the Holy Ghost. And by the power of the Holy Ghost ye may know the truth of all things." Most Mormons use these verses as a basis for their faith.

Most Mormons claim to have received a testimony as a result of following these instructions. They often refer to it as a "burning feeling" that told them the *Book of Mormon* is true. In the Mormon missionary lessons the potential convert is asked to read the *Book of Mormon* and then pray according to Moroni 10:4-5. The missionaries claim, "I know you will *feel* the truth of our message if you will make the effort to ponder these things and will seek the Lord in sincere prayer."[15]

The missionaries use the right word when they say *feel*. This plea is found in every missionary approach and the rest of the process of conversion into Mormonism depends on this feeling. There are Christians who have prayed sincerely and have received a feeling that the *Book of Mormon* is false. Who is to say which feeling, if either, came from God? One Utah pastor finds it helpful to ask a Mormon at the beginning of his witness to them, "In searching for God and truth, which is more dependable, the Bible or feelings?" Then he stresses the Bible's dependability with verses like "Heaven and earth shall pass away, but my words shall never pass away" (Mt 24:35). By contrast the danger of following feelings is expressed in Proverbs 14:12. "There is a way that *seems* right to a man, but in the end it leads to death." We must encourage Mormons to abandon this subjective basis for their faith and examine the *Book of Mormon* and Mormonism with their minds.

If you do not overcome this subjectivism, your efforts may be in vain. Many Mormons have been presented with mountains of evidence against the *Book of Mormon* and Mormonism only to respond, "But God has told me that it is true. There must be an answer to your claims." Sometimes it may take months or even years for a Mormon to abandon this subjectivism. Sandra Tanner was no exception. A few years after she left the Mormon Church she said, "It was a long time before I could admit I didn't believe the *Book of Mormon. . . .* It was weeks after that before I could say it out loud."[16]

What Should You Do Next?

If you have been successful up to this point—if you have created confidence in the Bible while creating doubts about the Mormon documents and emphasizing the subjective basis for Mormon faith—what should you do next? If God has used you to open the person's eyes, to create a desire to know the truth, then share Bible passages that teach sound Christian doctrine. Center your message on the person and work of Jesus Christ, making clear that he can provide forgiveness for all sins.

If possible, get your Mormon friend into a Bible study on basic Christian doctrine. Assume he has no correct understanding of any biblical concept unless he demonstrates he has. This is necessary to prevent his combining Mormon and Christian ideas. He needs to study subjects like the nature of God, the nature of sin, the person and work of Christ, salvation and conversion. In most cases it will take a long while for a Mormon to accept these teachings. Take your time, get into the Bible yourself and allow the Holy Spirit to work through you.

You can get help with Bible study from many sources. William York's *One to One* covers in succinct fashion the basics needed for someone to make a responsible commitment to Christ. A much more detailed outline of Christian doctrine that is still suitable for laypeople can be found in Bruce Milne's *Know the Truth* (Scripture references and study questions follow each section). John Stott's *Basic Christianity* is a classic introduction to the claims of Christ and their trustworthiness. Stott discusses the person and work of Christ, the nature of sin, and the necessary response. Paul Little's *How to Give Away Your Faith* makes general suggestions on how to witness, most of which you can readily adapt to witnessing to Mormons.[17]

Do not be discouraged if you are unable to involve your friend in a study of the Scriptures right away. Several months or years may pass before your witness bears fruit. Even though your witness seems to be having no effect, keep the communication lines open and keep sharing. Many times it will take a crisis in the life of a Mormon to make him realize that Mormonism is false.

I have a friend who spent nearly two years witnessing to a young Mormon businessman. Slowly he shared the problems with the Mormon scriptures, but his Mormon friend seemed unaffected. Evidently, though, the Mormon was beginning to have some doubts he did not share with anyone. As he began to doubt, his giving to the Church began to decrease. The more he doubted, the less he gave. Finally, his bishop called on him to see why he had not been giving his full tithe. That was the last straw. He asked the bishop to leave, called my friend and within two weeks gave his life to Christ.

Remember, the Mormons base their faith on a feeling. Often the facts a Christian presents seem to be ignored. But when a crisis comes, the subjectivism may not be enough to sustain the Mormon and he will call on a Christian friend for help and guidance.

In addition to information from the Bible, your personal testimony can have an effect. Mormons need to know that Christians have an experience with God. We must be careful, of course, to define our terms so our listener does not give them Mormon meanings.

I have also found it helpful not to refer to anything that a Mormon would consider anti-Mormon literature. A refutation of Mormon doctrine like the Tanners' *Mormonism: Shadow or Reality?* you should digest before the encounter. Your arguments will be more effective if you use Mormon books to refute Mormon doctrine.

Extremely useful are the reprints of the 1830 edition of the *Book of Mormon*, the 1833 edition of the *Book of Commandments* and the 1835 edition of the *Doctrine and Covenants*. These are published in two volumes by the Deseret News Press, the official Latter-day Saints Church press, under the title *Joseph Smith Begins His Work* by W. C. Wood and are thoroughly documented photoreproductions of the originals. They are distributed by Bookcraft Publishers Inc., Salt Lake City, Utah, on a wholesale basis. They are available on a retail basis in some Latter-day Saints bookstores and from Mission to Mormons, 1955 W. Hibbard Rd., Owosso, MI 48867. You can look up in these reprints the sections discussed in chapters two and four and compare them with current editions, available from Mormon missionaries or Latter-day Saints bookstores.

A final hint would be that it is not usually worthwhile to argue with a Mormon over controversial issues that have often been at the center of discussion in the past. Some of these are baptism for the dead, the stick of Joseph and the stick of Judah, the lifestyle and character of Joseph Smith, and polygamy. (Since we have not discussed many of these items in the body of this book, a brief description of them has been relegated to the glossary.) Such matters are not the primary problems. The main question is, Are three books—the *Book of Mormon*, the *Doctrine and Covenants*, and the *Pearl of Great Price*—really God's Word? Our conclusions on the rest of the disputed matters depend on our view of these books.

Witnessing to Mormons is not easy. Yet, because of the threat they pose to the body of Christ and because of our love for them, we must accept the responsibility of trying to help them see the truth.

Appendix A

Letter and Statement from the Smithsonian Institution, Department of Anthropology

Your recent inquiry concerning the Book of Mormon has been received in the Smithsonian's Department of Anthropology.

The Book of Mormon is a religious document and not a scientific guide. The Smithsonian Institution does not use it in archeological research. Because the Smithsonian Institution receives many inquiries regarding the Book of Mormon, we have prepared a "Statement Regarding the Book of Mormon," a copy of which is enclosed for your information. This statement includes answers to questions most commonly asked about the Book of Mormon.

Statement Regarding the Book of Mormon

1. The Smithsonian Institution has never used the Book of Mormon in any way as a scientific guide. Smithsonian archeologists see no connection between the archeology of the New World and the subject matter of the book.

2. The physical type of the American Indian is basically Mongoloid, being most closely related to that of the peoples of eastern, central, and northeastern Asia. Archeological evidence indicates that the ancestors of the present Indians came into the New World—probably over a land bridge known to have existed in the Bering Strait region during the last Ice Age—in a continuing series of small migrations beginning from about 25,000 to 30,000 years ago.

3. Present evidence indicates that the first people to reach this continent from the East were the Norsemen who briefly visited the northeastern part of North America around A.D. 1000 and then settled in Greenland. There is nothing to show that they reached Mexico or Central America.

4. One of the main lines of evidence supporting the scientific finding that contacts with Old World civilizations, if indeed they occurred at all, were of very little significance for the development of American Indian civilizations, is the fact that none of the principal Old World domesticated food plants or animals (except the dog) occurred in the New World in pre-Columbian times. American Indians had no wheat, barley, oats, millet, rice, cattle, pigs, chickens, horses, donkeys, camels before 1492. (Camels and horses were in the Americas, along with the bison, mammoth, and mastodon, but all these animals became extinct around 10,000 B.C. at the time when the early big

game hunters spread across the Americas.)

5. Iron, steel, glass, and silk were not used in the New World before 1492 (except for occasional use of unsmelted meteoric iron). Native copper was worked in various locations in pre-Columbian times, but true metallurgy was limited to southern Mexico and the Andean region, where its occurrence in late prehistoric times involved gold, silver, copper, and their alloys, but not iron.

6. There is a possibility that the spread of cultural traits across the Pacific to Mesoamerica and the northwestern coast of South America began several hundred years before the Christian era. However, any such inter-hemispheric contacts appear to have been the results of accidental voyages originating in eastern and southern Asia. It is by no means certain that even such contacts occurred; certainly there were no contacts with the ancient Egyptians, Hebrews, or other peoples of Western Asia and the Near East.

7. No reputable Egyptologist or other specialist on Old World archeology, and no expert on New World prehistory, has discovered or confirmed any relationship between archeological remains in Mexico and archeological remains in Egypt.

8. Reports of findings of ancient Egyptian, Hebrew, and other Old World writings in the New World in pre-Columbian contexts have frequently appeared in newspapers, magazines, and sensational books. None of these claims has stood up to examination by reputable scholars. No inscriptions using Old World forms of writing have been shown to have occurred in any part of the Americas before 1492 except for a few Norse rune stones which have been found in Greenland.

9. There are copies of the Book of Mormon in the library of the National Museum of Natural History, Smithsonian Institution.

Suggested Readings from the Smithsonian Institution

Coe, Michael D. *Mexico.* Revised edition. Thames & Hudson, 1982. (A well-written, authoritative summary of Mexican archeology.)

Coe, Michael D. *The Maya.* Revised edition. Thames & Hudson, 1980. (A general summary of the archeology of the Maya.)

Coe, Michael D. and Richard A. Diehl. *In the Land of the Olmec.* 2 vols. University of Texas Press, 1980.

Ferguson, Thomas S. *One Fold and One Shepherd.* San Francisco: Books of California, 1958. (A book presenting the Mormon point of view.)

Hammond, Norman. *Ancient Maya Civilization.* New Brunswick, New Jersey: Rutgers University Press, 1982.

Hunter, Milton R. and Thomas S. Ferguson. *Ancient America and the Book of Mormon.* Oakland, California: Kolob Book Co., 1950. (The Mormon point of view is presented.)

Jennings, Jesse D. *Prehistory of North America*. 2nd edition. McGraw-Hill, 1974.

Jennings, Jesse, editor. Vol. 1. *Ancient North Americans*. Vol. 2. *Ancient South Americans*. San Francisco: W. H. Freeman, 1983.

Jennings, Jesse D. and Edward Norbeck, editors. *Prehistoric Man in the New World*. University of Chicago Press, 1971. (A thorough survey of the field by 18 leading authorities, organized by geographical area.)

Kelley, David Humiston. *Deciphering the Maya Script*. Austin: University of Texas Press, 1976. (Comprehensive coverage of the subject.)

MacGowan, Kenneth and Joseph A. Hester, Jr. *Early Man in the New World*. Garden City, New Jersey: Anchor Books, Doubleday, 1962. (Good general reading; also provides some Old World background.)

Meggers, Betty J. *Prehistoric America*. Revised edition. Chicago: Aldine Press, 1977. (A short, single volume account written for the layman.)

Papers of the New World Archaeological Foundation. Provo, Utah: Brigham Young University, 1952-. (Published results of archeological investigations in Mesoamerica by the Foundation, supported by the Mormon Church.)

Riley, Carroll L. et al., editors. *Man Across the Sea: Problems of Pre-Columbian Contacts*. Austin: University of Texas Press, 1971. (A collection of articles, mostly by well-qualified specialists, concerning transoceanic contacts.)

Shutler, Richard, Jr., editor. *Early Man in the New World*. Beverly Hills, California: Sage Publications, 1983.

Thompson, J. Eric. *Maya Hieroglyphs Without Tears*. The British Museum, London. (An excellent introduction, briefer, simpler, and less up-to-date than the 1976 volume by Kelley listed above.)

Thompson, J. Eric. *The Rise and Fall of Maya Civilization*. 2nd enlarged edition. Norman: University of Oklahoma Press, 1977. (Reprint of 1954 edition.)

Wauchope, Robert. *Lost Tribes and Sunken Continents*. University of Chicago Press, 1974. (Chapter 4 covers Mormon theories, setting them in the context of other nonscientific schemes. Author is a well-qualified specialist on Mexican archeology.)

Willey, Gordon R. *An Introduction to American Archaeology*. Vol. I, North and Middle America (1966). Vol. II, South America (1971). Englewood Cliffs, New Jersey: Prentice-Hall, Inc.

Willey, Gordon, editor. *Pre-Columbian Archaeology: Readings from Scientific American*. San Francisco: W. H. Freeman, 1980.

Wolf, Eric. *Sons of the Shaking Earth*. University of Chicago Press, 1959. (A fine description of the prehistory and culture history of Mexico.)

Appendix B

Book of Mormon Passages Reflecting Christian Teaching or in Conflict with Mormon Doctrine

God Is Spirit

Alma 18:24-28 [LDS]*/12:103-106 [RLDS]

"there is a Great Spirit . . . This is God"

Alma 22:8-11/13:40-43

"Is God that Great Spirit . . . Yea"

Only One God †

Alma 11:28-39, 44/8:80-94, 104

Father, Son & Holy Ghost "one eternal God" is "the very eternal Father"

3 Nephi 11:25, 27, 36-40/5:25, 27, 38-42

baptize in name of Father, Son & Holy Ghost = in my name

Jesus is the Father & the Son

Mosiah 15:2-5/8:29-32

"becoming the Father and Son, And they are one God"

Mosiah 17:15/8:91

Christ "is the very Eternal Father"

Ether 3:14/1:77

"I am Jesus Christ, I am the Father and the Son"

Christ the Eternal God

2 Nephi 26:12/11:78

see also title page of Book of Mormon

2 Nephi 11:7/8:13-14

"if there be no Christ there be no God"

God Unchangeable

3 Nephi 24:6/11:9

"I am the Lord, I change not"

Moroni 7:22/7:21

"being from everlasting to everlasting"

Moroni 8:18/8:19

"he is unchangeable from all eternity to all eternity"

Mormon 9:9-10, 19/4:68-69, 81-82

"an unchangeable being," even in miracles

Man's Nature Sinful

Mosiah 3:19/1:119

"natural man is an enemy of God . . . will be forever"

---

* *Slash separates Utah Book of Mormon reference from the reference of the Reorganized Church's edition.*

† *While these passages do not reflect a full-fledged Trinitarian view of God, they do conflict with Mormon teaching that the Father, Son and Holy Ghost are three different gods.*

Ether 3:2/1:63

"because of the fall our natures have been evil continually"

Mosiah 16:3-4/8:74-76

"all mankind . . . carnal . . . endlessly lost"

2 Nephi 2:21/1:110

"all men . . . were lost because of the transgression of their parents"

Need Spiritual Birth

Alma 5:14/3:27-29

"have ye spiritually been born of God?"

Mosiah 27:24-28/11:186-190

"born of God, changed from their carnal fallen state"

3 Nephi 9:17/4:47

"as many as received me," quoting John 1:12

No Salvation after Death

Alma 34:32-35/16:228-234

"this life is the time," "this is the final state"

2 Nephi 28:21-23/12:25-29

"the devil . . . leadeth them away . . . to hell" no deliverance

2 Nephi 9:38/6:72

"those who die in their sins . . . remain in their sins"

1 Nephi 10:21/3:34-35

"sought to do wickedly . . . must be cast off forever"

Alma 40:11-14/19:42-47

"souls of the wicked . . . fearful looking for the wrath"

Alma 41:3-8/19:66-71

"evil . . . raised . . . to endless misery"

Mosiah 3:25-27/1:126-128

"endless torment, from whence they can no more return"

Mosiah 15:26/8:61-62

"willfully rebelled . . . no part in the first resurrection"

Mosiah 16:5/8:77-78

"persists in . . . carnal nature . . . as though . . . no redemption"

3 Nephi 27:11-22/12:23-35

"cast into the fire, from whence . . . no more return"

3 Nephi 27:33/13:11

"night cometh, wherein no man can work"

2 Nephi 28:22-23/12:28-29

"They are grasped with death and hell . . . must go into the place prepared for them, even a lake of fire"

Only Two Destinies

Mosiah 16:11/8:84

"if good, to the resurrection of endless life . . . if evil . . ."

Alma 5:39-42/3:64-70

"child of the devil . . . for his wages he receiveth death"

Alma 5:22-25/3:44-45

"guilty of all . . . wickedness . . . children of . . . the devil"

Alma 41:3-4/19:66-67

"raised to endless happiness . . . or to endless misery"

Helaman 12:26/4:73	some "consigned to a state of endless misery"
3 Nephi 26:5/11:33	"good to the resurrection of life . . . evil, to . . . damnation"

Torment Eternal

1 Nephi 14:3/3:208	"hell which hath no end"
2 Nephi 9:16/6:40	"their torment . . . has no end"
Mosiah 3:25/1:127	"torment, from whence . . . no . . . return"
Mosiah 5:5/3:6	"a never ending torment"

Smith's statement (DC 19:6/RDC 18:1) is not true that "It is not written that there shall be no end to this torment."

Salvation by Christ's Work, Not Man's

1 Nephi 10:6/3:6	"lost . . . ever would be, save they should rely on this Redeemer"
2 Nephi 25:23, 26/11:43–44, 48	"by grace . . . saved, after all we can do"
Jacob 7:12/5:21	"if . . . no atonement made all mankind must be lost"
Mosiah 3:17/1:116	"salvation can come . . . only in and through the name of Christ"
Mosiah 3:18/1:118	"salvation was, and is . . . through the atoning blood of Christ"
Mosiah 3:19/1:120	"becometh a saint through the atonement of Christ"
Mosiah 4:2–3/2:2–6	"apply the atoning blood of Christ that we may receive forgiveness"
Mosiah 4:6–8/2:10–11	"atonement . . . that thereby salvation might come to him . . . trust in the Lord"
Alma 21:9/13:13	"no redemption . . . save . . . through the death and sufferings of Christ"
Alma 34:8–16/16:207–217	"last sacrifice will be the Son of God . . . bring salvation to all those who . . . believe"
Helaman 5:9–12/2:71–75	"no means whereby . . . saved, only through the atoning blood of Jesus Christ"

Baptism Not Essential

Moroni 8:22/8:25–26	"all little children are alive in Christ, and also all they that are without the law . . . unto such baptism availeth nothing"
2 Nephi 31:13/13:16	"witnessing unto the Father that ye are willing to take upon you the name of Christ, by baptism" (see context)

Bible Contains the Gospel

Mormon 7:8/3:30   "the gospel of Christ . . . set before you . . . in
                                       the record which shall come unto the Gen-
                                       tiles from the Jews" (Bible)

Only One Priesthood (after Christ)

Moroni 2:1ff./2:1ff.   disciples—the twelve
Moroni 3:1-4/3:1-3   they ordained priests and teachers
Moroni 4:1/4:1-2   elders and priests ministered the sacra-
                                       ments
Alma 16:13/10:103   "consecrated . . . teachers . . . to baptize"

We are indebted to Pastor & Mrs. Gene Wilcox for sharing their compilation of verses.

A shortened version, "Divine Truths in the Book of Mormon," is available in tract form from Personal Freedom Outreach, Box 26062, St. Louis, MO 63136.

Appendix C

Cross-reference between Book of Commandments
and Doctrine and Covenants

The following is a chart comparing the revelations in the Book of Commandments with their counterparts in the Doctrine and Covenants. This chart is helpful because the order of the revelations have been changed several times. Fortunately there is an introductory paragraph with each revelation that makes it possible to compare them in each edition.

BC = *Book of Commandments*
DC = *Doctrine and Covenants*

1. BC 1, DC 1
2. DC 2, not in BC
3. BC 2, DC 3
4. BC 3, DC 4
5. BC 4, DC 5
6. BC 5, DC 6
7. BC 6, DC 7
8. BC 7, DC 8
9. BC 8, DC 9
10. BC 9, DC 10
11. BC 10, DC 11
12. BC 11, DC 12
13. DC 13, not in BC
14. BC 12, DC 14
15. BC 13, DC 15
16. BC 14, DC 16
17. DC 17, not in BC
18. BC 15, DC 18
19. BC 16, DC 19
20. BC 17—21, DC 23
21. BC 22, DC 21
22. BC 23, DC 22
23. BC 24, DC 20
24. BC 25, DC 24
25. BC 26, DC 25
26. BC 27, DC 26
27. BC 28, DC 27

28. BC 29, DC 29
29. BC 30, DC 28
30. BC 31—33, DC 30
31. BC 34, DC 31
32. DC 32, not in BC
33. BC 35, DC 33
34. BC 36, DC 34
35. BC 37, DC 35
36. BC 38, DC 36
37. BC 39, DC 37
38. BC 40, DC 38
39. BC 41, DC 39
40. BC 42, DC 40
41. BC 43, DC 41
42. BC 44, DC 42:1-73
43. BC 45, DC 43
44. BC 46, DC 44
45. BC 47, DC 42:74-93
46. BC 48, DC 45
47. BC 49, DC 46
48. BC 50, DC 47
49. BC 51, DC 48
50. BC 52, DC 49
51. BC 53, DC 50
52. DC 51, not in BC
53. BC 54, DC 52
54. BC 55, DC 53

55. BC 56, DC 54
56. BC 57, DC 55
57. BC 58, DC 56
58. DC 57, not in BC
59. BC 59, DC 58
60. BC 60, DC 59
61. BC 61, DC 60
62. BC 62, DC 61
63. BC 63, DC 62
64. BC 64, DC 63
65. BC 65, DC 64

Notes

Introduction
[1]Alexander Campbell, "Delusions," *Millennial Harbinger,* II, February 1831, p. 91.

Chapter 1
[1]*The Uniform System for Teaching Families* (Salt Lake City: Corp. of Pres. of Church of Jesus Christ of Latter-day Saints, 1973), p. C-31.

[2]Joseph Smith, *Journal of Discourses,* VI (Liverpool: Asa Calkin, 1859), p. 5.

[3]Ibid., pp. 3-4.

[4]Milton R. Hunter, *The Gospel through the Ages* (Salt Lake City: Deseret Book Co., 1958), p. 104.

[5]*Come unto Christ: Melchizedek Priesthood Personal Study Guide* (Salt Lake City: The Church of Jesus Christ of Latter-day Saints, 1984), p. 46.

[6]John A. Widtsoe, ed., *Discourses of Brigham Young* (Salt Lake City: Deseret Books, 1961), p. 227.

[7]Hunter, *The Gospel,* p. 113.

[8]W. Cleon Skousen, *The First 2,000 Years* (Salt Lake City: Bookcraft, 1979), p. 355.

[9]*Uniform System for Teaching Families,* pp. D-3, 5.

[10]Bruce McConkie, *Mormon Doctrine* (Salt Lake City: Bookcraft, 1958), p. 467.

[11]*Journal of Discourses,* I (Liverpool: F. D. Richards, 1855), p. 50.

[12]*Deseret News,* Church News Section, October 9, 1976, p. 11. However, Mormons who participate in the Temple Ceremonies are still told in the Lecture Before the Veil that Michael is "one of the Council of the Gods" and he "became the man Adam" (Larry Cozad's taped recording of the ceremony, Tape II).

[13]*Journal of Discourses,* I, 51.

[14]Joseph Fielding Smith, *Doctrines of Salvation* (Salt Lake City: Bookcraft, 1969), I, 19.

[15]*Journal of Discourses,* VIII (Liverpool: George Q. Cannon, 1861), p. 115.

[16]Orson Pratt, *The Seer* (Washington, D.C.: Orson Pratt, 1853), p. 158.

[17] *Uniform System for Teaching Families,* p. D–7.

[18] Ibid., pp. D–13, 17.

[19] Ibid., p. E–23.

[20] *Journal of Discourses,* IV (Liverpool: S. W. Richards, 1857), p. 54. On the practice of Blood Atonement see Jerald and Sandra Tanner, *The Mormon Kingdom* (Salt Lake City: Modern Microfilm Co., 1969), II, 134–69.

[21] Joseph Fielding Smith, *Teachings of the Prophet Joseph Smith* (Salt Lake City: Deseret Book Co., 1977), p. 327.

[22] James E. Talmage, *The Articles of Faith* (Salt Lake City: The Church of Jesus Christ of Latter-day Saints, 1977), p. 237.

[23] Parker Pratt Robinson, *Orson Pratt's Works* (Salt Lake City: Deseret News Press, 1945), p.196.

[24] Keith Marston, *Missionary Pal* (Salt Lake City: Publishers Press, 1959), pp. 73–75.

[25] Robinson, *Pratt's Works,* pp. 175–96. See also McConkie, *Mormon Doctrine,* pp. 129–30, where the Catholic Church is identified as the "church of the Devil" that removed the plain parts from the Bible.

Chapter 2

[1] Wesley P. Walters, *New Light on Mormon Origins* (La Mesa, Calif.: Utah Christian Tract Society, 1967), pp. 3ff. Revised and enlarged in *Dialogue: A Journal of Mormon Thought,* IV, No. I (Spring 1969): 60ff.

[2] The phrase is Fawn Brodie's.

[3] Fawn Brodie, *No Man Knows My History* (New York: Alfred A. Knopf. 1967), p. 67. For further evidence of the nineteenth-century environment reflected in the *Book of Mormon,* see Dan Vogel, *Indian Origins and the Book of Mormon* (Salt Lake City: Signature Books, 1986).

[4] Brodie, *No Man,* pp. 70–72.

[5] Ibid. Also, see Gordon Fraser, *What Does the Book of Mormon Teach?* (Chicago: Moody Press, 1964), pp. 86–91.

[6] Mormon 8:17, 9:32ff., Ether 12:22–28.

[7] Brodie, pp. 79–80, quoting Illinois Governor Ford's information.

[8] Whitmer interview in *The Hamiltonian* (Hamilton, Mo.) Jan 21, 1881, p. 4; Letter of *John Gilbert to J. T. Cobb,* Mar. 16, 1879, p. 5, quoting Harris's words to Gilbert (in New York Public Library, Schroeder Collection); Letter of *S. Burnett to Br. Johnson,* April 15, 1838, in *Joseph Smith Papers: Letter Book April 27, 1837—Feb. 9, 1843* (in Church Historian's Office, Salt Lake City) pp. 64–65. Burnett, hearing Harris make the latter statement at a public meeting felt the "last pedestal" of his faith give way and wrote this letter of resignation from the Church.

[9] George Arbaugh, *Revelation in Mormonism* (Chicago: University of Chicago Press, 1932), p. 9.

[10]Ibid.

[11]Lucy Mack Smith, *Biographical Sketches of Joseph Smith the Prophet and His Progenitors for Many Generations* (Liverpool: S. W. Richards, 1853), p. 85, as quoted in Hal Hougey, *"A Parallel"—The Basis of the Book of Mormon* (Concord, Calif.: Pacific Publishing Co., 1963), p. 5.

[12]B. H. Roberts, as reproduced in Hougey, *"A Parallel,"* pp. 7-20.

[13]See Roberts's full argumentation in B. H. Roberts, *Studies of the Book of Mormon* (Urbana & Chicago: University of Illinois Press, 1985).

[14]Hougey, *"A Parallel,"* p. 21.

[15]Joseph Smith, *The History of the Church of Jesus Christ of Latter-day Saints* (Salt Lake City: Deseret Book Co., 1972), IV, 461.

[16]Joseph Fielding Smith, *Doctrines of Salvation* (Salt Lake City: Bookcraft, 1954), I, 170.

[17]This quote is found in the journal of Oliver Huntington, III, p. 168 (typescript). He attended the meeting at which the statement by Joseph F. Smith was made. A typed copy of his journal is on deposit with the Utah State Historical Society. Photocopies are available.

[18]David Whitmer, *An Address to All Believers in Christ* (Concord, Calif.: Pacific Publishing Co., 1976), p. 12, a photo reproduction of the original 1887 printing.

[19]Jerald and Sandra Tanner, *Mormonism: Shadow or Reality?* (Salt Lake City: Modern Microfilm Co., 1982), p. 89. For a complete list of the changes in the *Book of Mormon* since the first edition, see Jerald and Sandra Tanner, *3,913 Changes in the Book of Mormon* (Salt Lake City: Modern Microfilm Co., 1965). This is a photoreproduction of the first edition of the *Book of Mormon* with the changes marked in the text. Also see William Brodie Crouch, *The Myth of Mormon Inspiration* (Shreveport, La.: Lamberts Book House, 1968), pp. 248-68.

[20]Tanner, *Mormonism,* p. 90.

[21]James E. Talmage, *Articles of Faith* (Salt Lake City: The Church of Jesus Christ of Latter-day Saints, 1977), pp. 466-67. Originally Joseph Smith regarded the Father as Jehovah. Brigham Young, with his teaching that Adam is our Father and God, called Michael (who became the man Adam) Jehovah. It was largely through the efforts of Apostles G. Q. Cannon and F. D. Richards that the LDS Church came to adopt its present position that the Son is Jehovah. See Boyd Kirkland "Jehovah as the Father" *Sunstone* 9, No. 2 (Autumn 1984): 36-44.

[22]Tanner, *Mormonism,* pp. 165-66.

[23]Ibid.

[24]Ibid.

[25]Francis W. Kirkham, *A New Witness for Christ in America, The Book of Mormon* (Independence, Mo.: Zion's Printing and Pub. Co., 1942), I, 200-201.

[26]Tanner, *Mormonism*, p. 90.

[27]Ibid. See also Sidney B. Sperry, *Answers to Book of Mormon Questions* (Salt Lake City: Book Craft, 1967), p. 203.

[28]Kirkham, pp. 199–201. See also B. H. Roberts, *Defense of the Faith* (Salt Lake City: Deseret News, 1907), I, 278–79.

Chapter 3

[1]Ross T. Christensen, *University Archaeological Society Newsletter*, 30 Jan. 1960, pp. 3–6.

[2]Michael Coe, "Mormons and Archaeology: An Outside View," in *Dialogue: A Journal on Mormon Thought*, 8, No. 2 (Summer 1973): 42.

[3]Ibid.

[4]Stanley B. Kimball, "Kinderhook Plates Brought to Joseph Smith Appear to Be a Nineteenth-Century Hoax," *The Ensign*, 11, No. 8 (August 1981): 66–74.

[5]Coe, *Dialogue*, p. 46.

[6]Address at the Sixth Annual Sunstone Theological Symposium, Salt Lake City, August 25, 1984, typed transcript, p. 31.

[7]Quoted in Hal Hougey, *Archaeology and the Book of Mormon* (Concord, Calif.: Pacific Publishing Co., 1976), pp. 6–7. Original article in *Dialogue: A Journal on Mormon Thought*, 1, No. 1 (Spring 1966): 145–246.

[8]Dee Green, "Book of Mormon Archaeology: The Myths and the Alternatives," in *Dialogue: A Journal on Mormon Thought*, 4, No. 2 (Summer 1969): 74. For some specific examples of misleading archaeological usages see, Martin Raisch, "All that Glitters: Uncovering Fool's Gold in Book of Mormon Archaeology," *Sunstone* 6, No. 1 (Jan.–Feb. 1981): 10–15.

[9]Milton R. Hunter, *Archaeology and the Book of Mormon* (Salt Lake City: Deseret Book Co., 1972), pp. 1–10.

[10]Dee Green, "Book of Mormon Archaeology," pp. 77–78.

[11]John L. Sorenson, "Ancient America and the Book of Mormon Revisited," in *Dialogue: A Journal on Mormon Thought*, 4, No. 2 (Summer 1969): 81.

[12]John L. Sorenson, *An Ancient American Setting for the Book of Mormon*, (Salt Lake City: Deseret Book Co., 1985).

[13]Deseret News, *Church News* 48, No. 30 (July 29, 1978): 16. For a penetrating analysis of the untenability of Sorenson's position see Dan Vogel's *Sunstone* paper, "The New Theory of Book of Mormon Geography: A Preliminary Examination," Sunstone Theological Symposium (August 23, 1986).

[14]Dee Green, "Book of Mormon Archaeology," p. 75.

[15]Ibid., p. 75, n. 13.

[16]Ibid., p. 80.

[17]Hal Hougey has done an excellent survey of all the pertinent information relating to the Lehi Tree of Life Stone in *The Truth about the "Lehi Tree-*

of-Life" Stone (Concord, Calif.: Pacific Publishing Co., 1963).

Chapter 4

[1]Arthur Budvarson, *Changes in Mormonism* (La Mesa, Calif.: Utah Christian Tract Society, n.d.), pp. 6–7.

[2]David Whitmer, *An Address to All Believers in Christ* (Richmond, Mo.: David Whitmer, 1887), pp. 54–55.

[3]Tanner, *Mormonism,* pp. 27–28.

[4]Sidney B. Sperry, *Doctrine and Covenants Compendium* (Salt Lake City: Bookcraft, 1960), p. 85.

[5]David Whitmer, in his *Address,* pp. 58–59, attributes these new doctrines and changes to the influence of Sidney Rigdon. See also F. M. McKiernan, *Sidney Rigdon 1792–1876* (Lawrence, Kans.: Coronado Press, 1972).

[6]Brodie, *No Man,* pp. 98–113. This section deals with the new society the Mormons built, the communal element, and Rigdon's influence. See also Arbaugh, *Revelation in Mormonism,* pp. 10ff.

[7]Whitmer, *Address,* p. 35.

[8]Tanner, *Mormonism,* p. 180.

[9]Joseph Fielding Smith, *Essentials in Church History* (Salt Lake City: Deseret Book Co., 1972). See chapters 22–26 for the history of this period. The First Presidency of the Church placed this book in libraries all over the world free of cost.

[10]Hyrum M. Smith, *Doctrine and Covenants Commentary* (Salt Lake City: Deseret Book Co., 1968), p. 497.

[11]Joseph Fielding Smith, *Answers to Gospel Questions* (Salt Lake City: Deseret Book Co., 1963), IV, 112. He argues that God "absolved" them from having to build the temple on the basis of DC 124:49–54.

[12]Tanner, *Mormonism,* p. 190.

[13]For an authoritative discussion on this verse from the Mormon view, see Smith, *Doctrine and Covenants Commentary,* p. 105.

[14]For more verses that support this view, see page 68, footnote u, in the 1961 edition of the *Book of Mormon.*

[15]*Uniform System,* F, pp. 25, 27, 31. On page 31 the first paragraph under "Concept 11" confirms the order taught by Mormon missionaries.

[16]Tanner, *Mormonism,* p. 30.

Chapter 5

[1]*Pearl of Great Price,* 1891 edition, p. iv.

[2]On the details of the acquisition see, Jay M. Todd, *The Saga of the Book of Abraham* (Salt Lake City: Deseret Book Co., 1969).

[3]LeGrand Richards, *A Marvelous Work and a Wonder* (Salt Lake City: Deseret Book Co., 1971), p. 427. Richards gives a good but brief account of the

history of the mummies and the papyri and of how they fell into the hands of Joseph Smith.

[4]Jerald and Sandra Tanner, *The Case Against Mormonism* (Salt Lake City: Modern Microfilm Co., 1968), II, 113.

[5]*Dialogue: A Journal of Mormon Thought* 3, No. 2 (Summer 1968): 73–84, 98–99; 3, No. 3 (Autumn 1968): 119–20, 130–32; Hugh Nibley, *The Message of the Joseph Smith Papyri* (Salt Lake City: Deseret Book Co., 1975), pp. 19–45.

[6]Tanner, *Mormonism*, p. 311. The Tanners have also been able to obtain photocopies of the original manuscript of the translation by Joseph Smith. These photocopies cover Abraham 1:1—2:18. (Tanner, *The Case Against Mormonism*, pp. 2:146–51). The translation is correlated with the Egyptian characters through three and a half lines of the "Small Sensen text."

[7]Photocopies of the original handwritten manuscripts of Joseph's "Translation" of the Book of Abraham can be found in H. Michael Marquardt, *The Joseph Smith Egyptian Papers* (Cullman, Ala.: Printing Service, 1981), pp. 146–88. The discussion that follows relies primarily on Tanner, *The Case Against Mormonism*, II.

[8]Klaus Baer, "The Breathing Permit of Hôr," *Dialogue*, 3, No. 3 (Autumn 1968): 119–20.

[9]Ibid., pp. 112–16, 133–34; Tanner, *Mormonism*, pp. 333–34.

[10]Baer, "Breathing Permit," pp. 126–27.

[11]For a translation of the readable parts of this hypocephalus see, Michael Dennis Rhodes, "A Translation and Commentary of the Joseph Smith Hypocephalus," *Brigham Young University Studies*, 17, No. 3 (Spring 1977): 265.

[12]Tanner, *Mormonism*, pp. 335–39; cf. also the detailed analysis by the Mormon Egyptologist Edward H. Ashment, "The Facsimilies of the Book of Abraham: A Reappraisal," *Sunstone* 4, Nos. 5 and 6 (Dec. 1979): 38–42.

[13]Tanner, *Mormonism*, pp. 335–39; cf. Rhodes, "A Translation," p. 263.

[14]Tanner, *Mormonism*, pp. 335–39.

[15]*Pearl of Great Price* (1981 ed.), facing Facsimile 2.

[16]Rhodes, "A Translation," pp. 259, 267–73.

[17]Ibid., pp. 265, 267–73.

[18]*Pearl of Great Price* (1981 ed.), under Facsimile 1.

[19]Richard A. Parker, "The Joseph Smith Papyri: A Preliminary Report," *Dialogue*, 3, No. 2 (Summer 1968): 86; Baer, "Breathing Permit," pp. 118–19. Cf. also the detailed analysis by Mr. Ashment of the incorrect restorations of the Facsimile in his "The Facsimilies," pp. 33–38.

[20]For a translation of these columns of characters see Baer, "Breathing Permit," pp. 116–17.

[21]*Pearl of Great Price* (1981 ed.), under Facsimile 3.

[22]Baer, "Breathing Permit," pp. 126-27.

[23]For a brief history of the Book of Abraham text, its acceptance as Scripture by the LDS and translations of the Egyptian texts related to the three Facsimilies see H. Michael Marquardt, "The Book of Abraham Revisited," *The Journal of Pastoral Practice,* 5, No. 4 (1982): 101-12.

[24]For various attempted rationalizations see Wesley P. Walters, "Joseph Smith Among the Egyptians," *Journal of the Evangelical Theological Society,* 16, No. 1 (Winter 1973): 25-45. Available in off-print from Utah Lighthouse Ministry, Salt Lake City.

[25]Hugh Nibley, *The Message,* p. 3. Cf. H. Michael Marquardt, *The Book of Abraham Papyrus Found,* rev. ed. (Salt Lake City, Utah, Modern Microfilm Co., 1981), p. 15.

[26]Baer, "Breathing Permit," pp. 110-16, 133-34.

[27]Ibid., pp. 111, 116-17, 119. For further evidence that the Sensen text was regarded by Joseph Smith as the Book of Abraham see H. Michael Marquardt, *The Book of Abraham Papyrus Found;* Marquardt, "Book of Abraham Revisited" and Wesley P. Walters's book review, *Journal of Pastoral Practice,* 5, No. 4 (1982): 118-20.

[28]Edward H. Ashment, "Dealing with Dissonance: The Book of Abraham as a Case Study," Sunstone Theological Symposium, August 24, 1984.

[29]Ibid., Dr. Hugh Nibley, *Abraham in Egypt* (Salt Lake City: Deseret Book Co., 1981) has even suggested that Joseph could have received the entire "translation" by revelation since Joseph "had already demonstrated at great length his power to translate ancient records with or without possession of the original text" (p. 4).

[30]Letter, Thomas Stuart Ferguson to James Boyack, March 13, 1971.

Chapter 6

[1]John L. Smith, *Witnessing Effectively to Mormons* (Marlow, Okla.: Utah Missions Inc., 1975), pp. 29-30.

[2]Geisler and Nix, *A General Introduction to the Bible* (Chicago: Moody Press, 1968), p. 263.

[3]Gleason Archer, *A Survey of Old Testament Introduction* (Chicago: Moody Press, 1974), p. 25.

[4]Quoted in Josh McDowell, *Evidence That Demands a Verdict* (Campus Crusade For Christ International, 1972), pp. 56-57.

[5]Geisler and Nix, *General Introduction,* p. 361.

[6]F. F. Bruce, *The New Testament Documents: Are They Reliable?* (Downers Grove, Ill.: InterVarsity Press, 1960), p. 19.

[7]Brooke Foss Westcott and Fenton John Anthony Hort, ed., *The New Testament in the Original Greek* (New York and London: Harper & Brothers, 1898), p. 561.

[8]Bruce, *New Testament Documents,* pp. 16–18; J. A. Thompson, *The Bible and Archaeology* (Grand Rapids: Eerdmans, 1962), p. 437.

[9]Quoted in McDowell, *Evidence,* p. 44.

[10]Quoted in Bruce, *New Testament Documents,* p. 20.

[11]Milton Hunter, in his book *The Gospel through the Ages,* explains this doctrine fully:

> In the first stage, man was an eternally existent being termed an intelligence. The next realm where man dwelt was the spirit world. According to Mormon concept eternally-existing intelligences were clothed with spirit bodies in the mansion of their Eternal Father. . . . [They are] born of heavenly parents into that eternal family in the spirit world. . . . There in the spirit world they were reared to maturity, becoming grown spirit men and women prior to coming upon this earth. . . . Here he receives a physical body and undergoes the experiences of mortality. . . . Eventually, however, mortal death comes upon all. This eternal spirit goes to the spirit world to await resurrection and judgment. . . . There some of them will become Angels, and others priests and Kings, or in other words Gods. (Hunter, *Gospel,* pp. 126–29)

Hunter further states that progression applies to God: "Our Eternal Father has attained His position of exaltation and Godhood by obedience to the great law of progression" (Hunter, *Gospel,* p. 12).

[12]Just how the Book of Mormon people were able to "read" these verses from Hebrews 13:8 and James 1:17 here in America 500 years before the Spaniards brought the New Testament to this continent has not been successfully explained by Mormon writers.

[13]Joseph Fielding Smith, *Teachings of the Prophet Joseph Smith* (Salt Lake City: Deseret Book Co., 1977), p. 345.

[14]Although this is the traditional position of the Mormon Church, Mormons today are being taught that God's progression consists only of an increase in the number of children he produces. Nevertheless, Mormons still believe God has changed from an intelligence, to a spirit-person, to a man, to a god.

[15]*Uniform System for Teaching Families,* pp. C-27–29. (Emphasis added.)

[16]Interview in Wallace Tanner, *The Mormon Establishment* (Boston: Houghton Mifflin Co., 1966), p. 156.

[17]All of the titles mentioned in this paragraph are available from InterVarsity Press.

Glossary of Mormon Terms

Many Mormon terms have not been mentioned or discussed at length in this book because they are not essential for an effective witness to Mormons. We define several of them here in case you come upon them in your conversation or reading and need to know their meaning. The meaning given is the Mormon, not the Christian, one.

Apostle: one of the twelve men who serve under the First Presidency. They have various responsibilities within the Mormon Church, such as missions, visitor centers, finances.

Apostate: one who has left the Mormon Church.

Baptism for the Dead: immersion in water on behalf of a deceased person, who can accept or reject its benefit. The Mormons have nearly five billion names on microfilm in their genealogical records so that church members can search out their ancestors and be baptized for them. This doctrine is based on an incorrect understanding of 1 Corinthians 15:29.

Bishop: the nonpaid leader of a Mormon ward, the closest parallel to a Christian minister.

Branch: a Mormon congregation not large enough to be called a ward; a mission congregation.

Chapel: a ward meetinghouse.

Church: Mormonism; the Mormon headquarters in Salt Lake City.

Deacon: an office given to Mormon boys at age 12.

Elder: a relatively minor office in the Mormon Church held by Mormon missionaries and other men. More influential officers who are not bishops, even apostles, may be referred to as elders.

Endowments: a secret ceremony revealing information and powers to priesthood holders. It takes place in a temple prior to eternal marriage or the sending out of a missionary to a foreign field.

First Presidency: the Mormon Prophet, or President, and his two counselors.

General Authorities: the First Presidency and Apostles.

Gentile: any non-Mormon.

Institute of Religion: the Mormon college and university ministry; a free educational program used by Mormons to attract converts on the campuses. These programs are becoming widespread throughout the United States.

M. I. A.: Mutual Improvement Association, the Mormon youth organization.

Negro Doctrine: the Mormon teaching that Blacks could not hold the priesthood because they were sinful in their pre-existent state; therefore, God had cursed them with a black skin. Since they were denied the priesthood, it was taught that they could not be saved to the highest degree of the Mormon Heaven. This doctrine came from the Book of Abraham and was supposed to have been recorded on a portion of the papyrus where there was a hole in the document and the missing characters were supplied from Joseph's imagination. In 1978 this Negro doctrine was abolished.

Patriarchal Blessing: a prophecy concerning the future of a young, faithful Mormon given by one of the older men in each congregation called a Ward Patriarch. The office of Patriarch over the entire church was recently abolished.

Polygamy: the practice of having more than one wife, either in this life or in the life to come. See *Doctrine and Covenants,* section 132.

Priesthood: the authority to act for God. Nearly every male Mormon from 12 years old on up is said to hold the priesthood.

Primary: the Mormon organization for grade-school children.

Relief Society: the Mormon women's organization.

Sacrament: communion or the Lord's Supper. Mormons use water and light bread as the elements.

Saints: Mormons.

Seminary: an educational program on the high-school level. Often adjacent to the public schools in the west, the teachers usually have a current state certificate and are paid according to public school pay scales.

Stake: a geographic area with several wards.

The "Stick of Joseph" and the "Stick of Judah": the *Book of Mormon* and the Bible respectively. These labels are based on a false interpretation of Ezekiel 37:18-23.

Temple: a building in which Mormons perform secret ceremonies, eternal marriages and baptisms for the dead. As of January 1987 the Mormons have forty temples in use throughout the world with three further temples under construction and another four announced for future construction. Only Mormons in good standing may enter a temple.

Ward: a local Mormon congregation.

Word of Wisdom: section 89 in the *Doctrine and Covenants,* which forbids the use of "hot drinks" (coffee and tea), tobacco and alcohol.

Selected and Annotated Bibliography

This bibliography includes the most important items for further study from both Mormon and non-Mormon sources. Some of these books are available in Christian bookstores. Others are difficult to find and may be ordered from Mission to Mormons. For current prices and an order form, write to Mission to Mormons, 1955 W. Hibbard Rd., Owosso, MI 48867.

Non-Mormon Publications

Barnett, Maurice. *Mormonism Against Itself,* 2 vols., Louisville, Ky.: Gospel Anchor Publishing Co., 1980. A collection of hard-to-find quotations, photo-reproduced from Mormon books and documents, in full context. Arranged by topics and printed on one side only of three-ring punched 8½″ X 11″ sheets (back of each page kept blank for lecture and personal notes). Available from the publisher at 712 Victoria Place, Louisville, KY 40207.

Brodie, Fawn M. *No Man Knows My History.* New York: Alfred A. Knopf, 1967. The best biography of Joseph Smith. Brodie was excommunicated from the Mormon Church for writing it.

Bruce, F. F. *The New Testament Documents: Are They Reliable?* Downers Grove, Ill.: InterVarsity Press, 1973. An extremely helpful book for supporting the accuracy of the New Testament.

Crouch, William Brodie. *The Myth of Mormon Inspiration.* Shreveport, La.: Lambert Book House, n.d. A carefully reasoned examination of Mormon inspiration.

Geer, Thelma. *Mormonism, Mama & Me.* Revised & enlarged ed. Chicago: Moody Press, 1986. A warm and loving presentation of Mormon life and doctrine by the great-granddaughter of John D. Lee. Her discovery of the Savior and her deep love for him sweeten the careful documentation of the book.

Hoekema, Anthony A. *The Four Major Cults.* Grand Rapids: Eerdmans, 1970. A work whose section on Mormonism is very valuable. Also contains extensive bibliography both pro and con.

Hougey, Hal. *Archaeology and the Book of Mormon.* Concord, Calif.: Pacific Publishing Co., 1975. An inexpensive booklet that covers the topic well.

McDowell, Josh. *Evidence That Demands a Verdict.* Campus Crusade for Christ, 1972. An apologetic containing much material about the reasons for our confidence in both the New and Old Testaments.

Mysteries of the Ancient Americas. Pleasantville, N.Y.: The Reader's Digest Association, 1986. A pictorial and narrative presentation of the latest scholarship on the origins of man in the Americas.

Ships, Jan. *Mormonism: The Story of a New Religious Tradition.* Urbana and Chicago: University of Illinois Press, 1985. A favorable appraisal of Joseph Smith, supporting the view that Mormonism should be regarded as a new religion and not just an extension of Christianity.

Tanner, Jerald and Sandra. *The Changing World of Mormonism.* Chicago: Moody Press, 1980. A shorter, more popular and easy-to-read version of their more encyclopedic work, *Mormonism: Shadow or Reality?* The Tanners, former Mormons, have written over thirty books and pamphlets that are available directly from them at Box 1884, Salt Lake City, UT 84110.

Tanner, Jerald and Sandra. *Mormonism: Shadow or Reality?* Salt Lake City: Utah Lighthouse Mission, 1982. The most extensive reference work available on Mormonism (nearly six hundred pages). The Tanners, former Mormons, have written over thirty books and pamphlets that are available directly from them at Box 1884, Salt Lake City, UT 84110.

Vogel, Dan. *Indian Origins and the Book of Mormon.* Salt Lake City: Signature Books, 1986. Traces the issues current in the pre-1830 period and how these issues (no longer occupying our attention today) influenced the writing of the *Book of Mormon.*

Where Does It Say That? Brockton, Mass.: Ex-Mormons for Jesus, 1986. Nearly two hundred pages of photoreproductions of early Mormon literature showing doctrines which have been modified or abandoned. This material is otherwise extremely difficult or expensive to obtain. Write Ex-Mormons for Jesus, P.O. Box 2403, Brockton, MA 02403.

Mormon Publications

Arrington, Leonard, and Bitton, Davis. *The Mormon Experience.* New York: Alfred A. Knopf, 1979. An overview of Mormonism, partly topical in arrangement, by the former LDS Church Historian and Assistant Historian.

Book of Mormon. Salt Lake City: Church of Jesus Christ of Latter-day Saints, 1961.

Doctrine and Covenants/Pearl of Great Price. Salt Lake City: Church of Jesus Christ of Latter-day Saints, 1968.

Hill, Donna. *Joseph Smith: The First Mormon.* Garden City, N.Y.: Doubleday & Co., 1977. A biography of Joseph Smith that attempts to be friendly yet open to recent research and some newly available church archival materials.

Hinkley, Gordon B. *Truth Restored.* Salt Lake City: Church of Jesus Christ of Latter-day Saints, 1969. A short history of the Mormon Church as told by a Latter-day Saints Apostle.

Howard, Richard P. *Restoration Scriptures: A Study of their Textual Development.* Independence, Mo.: Herald Publishing House, 1969. An objective study of the manuscript texts from which the printed Mormon Scriptures were derived. This important study by the Church Historian of the Reorganized Church led the way for a more scholarly handling of Mormon history.

McConkie, Bruce R. *Mormon Doctrine.* 2nd. ed. Salt Lake City: Bookcraft, 1979. An alphabetical arrangement of Mormon theology as set forth by a heading Mormon Apostle, recently deceased. A basic reference work.

Richards, LeGrand. *A Marvelous Work and a Wonder.* Salt Lake City: Deseret News Press, 1971. A work designed to help a Mormon missionary with his apologetics.

Roberts, B. H. *Studies of the Book of Mormon.* Urbana and Chicago: University of Illinois Press, 1985. A private work of B. H. Roberts, arguing for the human origin of the Book of Mormon. Kept privately by his family for many years, the volume was edited and published by Mormon scholars Brigham D. Madsen and Sterling M. McMurrin.

Sorenson, John L. *An Ancient Setting for the Book of Mormon.* Salt Lake City: Deseret Book Co., 1985. A Mormon scholar's attempt to limit *Book of Mormon* lands to Southern Mexico.

Talmage, James E. *Study of the Articles of Faith.* Salt Lake City: Church of Jesus Christ of Latter-day Saints, 1968. A discussion of the primary Mormon doctrines.

Walker, John Phillip, editor. *Dale Morgan on Early Mormonism.* Salt Lake City: Signature Books, 1986. A reappraisal of Mormon origins by a renowned American historian of Mormon heritage. These early chapters of a larger and uncompleted history have been ably edited, along with key selections from Morgan's voluminous correspondence. An important contribution to Mormon studies.

Wirth, Diane E. *A Challenge to the Critics: Scholarly Evidences of the Book of Mormon.* Bountiful, Utah: Horizon Publishers, 1986. A handy summary of the current Mormon arguments used to counter the Smithsonian Institution's statements and to defend the book of Mormon. Her heavy dependence on the scholarship of Brigham Young University writers undercuts the validity of many of her points.

Wood, Wilford C. *Joseph Smith Begins His Work.* 2 vols. Salt Lake City: Deseret News Press, 1963. Valuable photoreprints of the 1830 edition of the *Book of Mormon,* the 1833 edition of the *Book of Commandments* and the 1835 edition of the *Doctrine and Covenants.*

About the Author

Harry L. Ropp (A.B., Taylor University, 1969; M.A. and M.Div. in doctrine and philosophy, Lincoln Christian Seminary, Lincoln, Illinois, 1974) was director of Mission to Mormons until his death in 1978. The bulk of his M.A. work dealt with the Mormon doctrine of revelation. This book is an expansion of his masters thesis. Prior to founding the mission (now called the Intermountain Evangelizing Association, Inc.), Harry Ropp ministered to churches in Indiana and Illinois. Since his death, the work of the mission continues, with staff holding workshops and seminars for churches and college groups across the country. Through these workshops they seek to stem the flow of converts from Christian churches to Mormonism and help Christians witness effectively to Mormons. Questions about these workshops and any correspondence concerning Mormonism may be addressed to: Intermountain Evangelizing Association, or Mission to Mormons, 1955 W. Hibbard Road, Owosso, MI 48867.